J. MASON BREWER,

FOLKLORIST AND SCHOLAR:

HIS EARLY TEXAS WRITINGS

J. MASON BREWER, FOLKLORIST AND SCHOLAR: HIS EARLY TEXAS WRITINGS

Edited by
Bruce A. Glasrud and Milton S. Jordan

Foreword by
Kenneth L. Untiedt

STEPHEN F. AUSTIN STATE UNIVERSITY PRESS

Copyright ©2016 by Bruce A. Glasrud and Milton S. Jordan

All rights reserved. Printed in the United States of America. No part of this book may be used or reproduced in any manner whatsoever without the writer's permission except in the case of brief quotations in critical articles or reviews.

For more information:
Stephen F. Austin State University Press
P.O. Box 13007 SFA Station
Nacogdoches, Texas 75962
sfapress@sfasu.edu
www.sfasu.edu/sfapress

Book design: Shaina Hawkins
Cover design: Shaina Hawkins
Distributed by Texas A&M Consortium
www.tamupress.com

LIBRARY OF CONGRESS CATALOGING-IN-PUBLICATION DATA
Glasrud, Bruce A. and Jordan, Milton S.
J. Mason Brewer/Bruce A. Glasrud and Milton S. Jordan
ISBN: 978-1-62288-134-5

TABLE OF CONTENTS

FOREWORD 5
    Kenneth L. Untiedt
ACKNOWLEDGMENTS 9
INTRODUCTION 11
    J. Mason Brewer: Folklorist, Historian, Poet
    Bruce A. Glasrud and Milton S. Jordan
PUBLICATIONS/CONTRIBUTIONS
1. "Me and Jim Myers" 27
    J. H. Brewer
2. *Glimpses of Life: Poems* 33
    J. Mason Brewer
3. *The Negro in Texas History* 73
    J. Mason Brewer
4. *Heralding Dawn: An Anthology of Verse by Texas Negroes* 91
    J. Mason Brewer
5. *The Life of John Wesley Anderson in Verse* 146
    J. Mason Brewer
6. "John Tales" 196
    J. Mason Brewer
7. *More Truth Than Poetry* 222
    J. Mason Brewer

BIBLIOGRAPHY 249

FOREWORD

African American scholar J. Mason Brewer's name is commonly known in the Texas Folklore Society, but even there, our members probably don't know as much about him as they should. Why do I say that? Well, let me explain by saying that when I think of Mason Brewer, I recall a story told by one of our members, Jack Duncan, who shared his memories of prominent TFS members he'd met and come to respect throughout his years in the Society ("Under the Influence," *Celebrating 100 Years*, PTFS LXVI). He said he once heard Brewer give a banquet address and, after listening for a few minutes, Jack realized that Brewer was giving the presentation in rhymed verse, and he went on to speak effortlessly for about thirty minutes—with apparently no notes. Wow! I don't know anyone who would even attempt such a challenge anymore.

Who was Mason Brewer? He was a teacher, an administrator, a proponent for racial equality, a scholar, a writer...a folklorist. That doesn't tell enough, though. In each of these areas, he embodied diversity, and this book evidences that through presenting a variety of his many publications. This collection of works is clearly not a biography. Indeed, Bruce Glasrud and Milton Jordan emphasize that such a work has yet to be written. Their Introduction overviews Brewer's influences, interests, and impressive accomplishments. He came from a family of educators—either in the formal sense (his mother spent five decades as a school teacher), or indirectly (his father was a storyteller, who shared tales from his own assorted occupations and life experiences, shaping his son's interest in the oral tradition and recording cultural elements that otherwise would have been lost). Brewer's interest in academia and, specifically, in folklore studies, was thereby molded from the very beginning. He understood that folklore has many facets, and, like life in general, there is no linear path to discovering the essence of what defines a person, or a culture.

Brewer enlisted during WWI, utilizing his knowledge of three languages to serve as a translator. After his military service and then completing undergraduate work, he eventually settled into a teaching career. As an educator, he was an admired teacher, but also an effective administrator, using his renown to appeal to other notable scholars and personalities to speak to students at institutions where he taught. Despite the limitations put on African Americans during the era, he was among the first black educators to teach at any universities in Texas during the late '60s, having established himself as a prominent scholar in folklore studies. He was the first African American in several major academic organizations, gaining acceptance through his undeniable knowledge and skills as a researcher, teacher, and speaker. As a writer, Brewer published creative works in poetry and short fiction, as well as abundant historical and biographical research.

He is ranked among the most important of black folklorists of the twentieth century, with the likes of well-known writer Zora Neale Hurston. His national esteem did well to bring attention to other black scholars, and also to the Texas Folklore Society—and folklore study in general. Brewer joined the TFS in 1932, our first African-American member. He had received a graduate degree from Indiana University, studying under Stith Thompson, who had himself established his place in the Society by putting together the first Publication of the Texas Folklore Society (later titled *Round the Levee*). Brewer began making contributions immediately, at meetings and in our publications, but he did not merely want to collect stories, poems, and tales; he analyzed and classified them, without removing the authenticity of the people from which they originated. His published findings earned him honorary doctoral degrees and many other accolades, not only from the Texas Folklore Society's most prominent members, but from scholars everywhere.

Bruce Glasrud has contributed to the Texas Folklore Society through presentations at meetings and in our publications, and he is a former Councilor on the Society's Board; he has written extensively about African American heritage, publishing books specifically about African Americans in Texas and the South. Milton Jordan has studied East Texas history as told through stories of "the folk," as well as African American issues and civil rights, working previously with Glasrud on *Free Blacks in Antebellum Texas*. Both are active in and speak at various historical organizations throughout Texas, and their research emphasizes the significance of oral history in defining culture. In this book Glasrud and Jordan provide a brief biographical Introduction, along with several representative selections of the impressive body of work J. Mason Brewer produced. The selections demonstrate Brewer's seemingly disparate interests, from his poetry to historical writings, to his focus on folklore—of African Americans as well as other cultures to show how the influences are integrated. Ultimately, Brewer wanted to preserve and share the black culture with others, but his interests were certainly not limited in the types of works he wrote. This book presents a means for examination of the flavor of each area of his written repertoire.

J. Mason Brewer's ability to accurately capture the stories, beliefs, and dialect of African Americans is unquestionably a monumental contribution to literary scholarship. While folklore scholarship may not be as prominent as it once was in American universities (or other academic circles), Brewer went beyond—and the information he recorded about his culture and those that influenced it is still important. More research can be done by studying the stories, people, and cultures about which he wrote. This book provides a sampling of the materials published by Brewer that have yet to be researched.

—Kenneth L. Untiedt
Secretary-Editor, Texas Folklore Society
Nacogdoches, Texas

ACKNOWLEDGMENTS

A large and rich collection of material by and about J. Mason Brewer is housed in the James Gee Library at Texas A&M University, Commerce. This material is located in part at the general Library collection but primarily in the Special Collections and Archives. Faculty, staff and students at the University have been of great help in our effort to collect these early Texas writings of Brewer. The Special Collections Librarian, Andrea Weddle, has been unfailing in her assistance and generous in her spirit. Archivist Michael Barera was helpful and consistently prompt in reply to our repeated inquiries. Professor Jessica Brannon-Wranosky and several of her students at A&M Commerce put the Brewer Collection into organized and useful order and regularly found things we had overlooked. Without the help of these individuals we would not have been able to begin or complete this collection.

Dr. Joe Pierce of San Antonio graciously invited us to look over his collection of Brewer first editions and other rarities and shared with us his bibliographies listing most of Brewer's writings. Dr. Pierce and his wife Aaronetta have what is surely one of the most important collections of art and literature by Texas African Americans to be found anywhere. Dr. Pierce also put us in touch with Brewer's niece, Minnie M. Miles, who over a pleasant cup, or two, of coffee shared with us her memories of "Uncle Mason" and her informed thoughts on the significance of his work. We are especially grateful to Ms. Miles who on behalf of Brewer's family granted us permission to reprint the works of her uncle that are included in this book.

The staffs at the Dolph Briscoe Center for American History and the Harry Ransom Humanities Research Center at the University of Texas were consistently helpful in finding copies of scarce Brewer publications. Brenda Gunn, Director of Research & Collections, was one individual at the Briscoe CAH who enabled us to locate our materials. Working at the Texas State Library was a superb treat; we thank the staff for the courtesy presented to us. The archival and library staff at University of Texas at San Antonio located and provided us with a copy of Brewer's scarce 1936 publication, *The Negro in Texas History*. Shari Salisbury at UTSA provided Glasrud with information about *The Negro in Texas History*. We further were aided and abetted in our quest by scholars/friends Kay Arnold, Scott Sosebee, Mary Lenn Dixon, Ronald Chrisman, Dan Utley, Gwendolyn Lawe, and Cary Wintz.

At least five other colleagues helped us with this book. Texas State University student and East Foundation employee, Kristine Robb, helped us with scanning and editing. The first rate Foreword was written by Kenneth L. Untiedt, professor of English at Stephen F. Austin State University and Executive Secretary of the Texas Folklore Society. Many, many thanks, Ken. Kim Verhines, editor and director of the Stephen F. Austin State University Press, reviewed our proposal, made a quick and positive decision and told us what she would need. With the extensive design and editorial work of Shaina G. Hawkins they produced this collection of the lesser known works of J. Mason Brewer. We are grateful for their good help. As often is the case, Anne Elton Jordan and Pearlene Vestal Glasrud read, edited, and supported our effort. Thanks Anne and Pearlene. We remain responsible for any errors or omissions.

–*Bruce A. Glasrud, San Antonio, Texas*
–*Milton S. Jordan, Georgetown, Texas*

INTRODUCTION

J. MASON BREWER: FOLKLORIST, HISTORIAN, POET

In the fall of 1969 African American scholar J. Mason Brewer was named Visiting Distinguished Professor at East Texas State University, now Texas A&M University Commerce, where he remained until his death in 1975. Brewer accepted the appointment after a successful career teaching in the public schools and public and private colleges of Texas and following ten years as Professor of English at Livingstone College, an historically black private school in Salisbury, North Carolina. Brewer, and David A. Talbot, also appointed as a faculty member at East Texas State University in 1969, were the first African American professors at the university in Commerce.[1] They were among the earliest black faculty at any of Texas' previously all-white segregated colleges and universities, especially those in the eastern part of the state. This path-breaking achievement was far from being the first of the pioneering appointments, honors, and memberships in Brewer's long life and career.

John Mason Brewer, known as Mason to family and friends, was born March 24, 1896, in Goliad, Texas. His parents, J. H. and Minnie T. Brewer, were significant influences on his career as an educator and kindled his lifelong interest in the folklore of African Americans. Brewer's mother taught in Texas segregated public schools for fifty years and encouraged Brewer to read black authors as well as to explore African American history. His father, given the social and economic realities of late 19th and early 20th century Texas, was employed variously as a wagoner, cowhand, mail carrier, and grocer although during the twentieth century he principally worked as a barber until his death in 1961. The elder Brewer's tales and stories of these varied experiences created and encouraged Mason's interest in folklore.[2] One such story that J. H. Brewer told his son (and that Mason wrote down), "Me and Jim Myers," is included as the first selection in our book, *J. Mason Brewer, Folklorist and Scholar*, a story that Brewer also published under a different title, "A Negro Cowboy."[3]

J. Mason Brewer finished high school in Austin, Texas and graduated from Wiley College in Marshall, Texas in 1917 with a bachelor's degree in English. He returned to Austin to teach for one year and then joined the U.S. Army during the First World War. Brewer was stationed in France and fluent in French and Spanish, he served as a translator with the rank of Corporal.[4] Returning from his military service Brewer taught for five years in the Fort Worth public schools. While there he published *Echoes of Thought* and *Glimpses of Life*, books of poetry published by the Progressive Printing Company of Fort Worth. *Glimpses of Life* is the second of Brewer's works included in *J. Mason Brewer, Folklorist and Scholar*.[5]

Brewer then moved to Colorado where he worked in Denver for a year for the Continental Oil Company. He continued writing and in Colorado he published stories and poems in the company magazine and in the periodical, *The Negro American*. Preferring to teach, Brewer returned to Austin in 1926 as a professor at Samuel Huston College where he taught in the languages department. While in Austin, at the suggestion of University of Texas scholar, J. Frank Dobie, Brewer turned his attention from poetry to the collecting and preserving of folklore.[6]

Brewer continued teaching, but as a young instructor/teacher, he lived in several communities. In the thirties he moved to Dallas where he taught English and Spanish at Booker T. Washington High School, and frequently involved his students in research and writing projects such as a book of poetry, *Patriotic Moments: A Second Book of Verse*, and a collaborative history titled *A History of the Dallas High School for Negroes*.⁷ During World War II Brewer taught for a year at Claflin College in South Carolina. In 1943, returning from Claflin College, Brewer was named chair of the Department of English Language and Literature at the newly merged Huston-Tillotson College (now University) where he remained until 1959.⁸

In these productive years Brewer wrote and edited over fifteen books of poetry, history and biography as well as producing his own collections of folklore. Brewer was adept at teaching his students to write and edit, and a few of his publications are collections of their materials. In the 1930s Brewer's own publications included *Negrito: Negro Dialect Poems from the Southwest*; a brief guidebook for the Texas Centennial, *The Negro in Texas History*; and an important collection of Texas African American poetry, *Heralding Dawn: An Anthology of Verse by Texas Negroes*. Brewer's most significant historical writing, *Negro Legislators of Texas: A History of Negroes in Texas Politics from Reconstruction to Disfranchisement* was published in 1935 by the Dallas firm, Mathis Publishing.⁹ Both *The Negro in Texas History* (number three) and *Heralding Dawn* (number four) are included as selections in this book. In his publications Brewer successfully sought to portray black life and culture.

That interest led Brewer to the study of African American folklore which would be his major contribution to United States literature. Lacking a graduate degree, although he earlier had taken graduate courses at the University of Denver and the University of Colorado, Brewer enrolled at Indiana University where he studied folklore with Stith Thompson and where he earned his master's degree in 1933. In Thompson's courses, especially "The Folktale and Allied

Forms," Brewer gained confirmation of his conviction that the tales and stories he had grown up hearing, and was now collecting, were significant and worthy of preserving. In 1951, Paul Quinn College in Waco awarded Brewer the honorary degree Doctor of Literature for his unmatched contribution to African American literature and folklore.[10] Adding to the folklore that Brewer already had collected and published with the Texas Folklore Society, in 1953 Brewer published his first major folklore collection, *The Word on the Brazos: Negro Preacher Tales from the Brazos Bottoms of Texas*. Dedicated to his grandfathers and father, the book included an "Introduction" by University of Texas scholar J. Frank Dobie.[11]

Brewer earlier met Dobie when each was teaching at Austin colleges separated by a few blocks and the deep chasm of Texas racial segregation. In 1932 Brewer crossed at least the few blocks and delivered to Dobie, then editor and secretary of the Texas Folklore Society, a box filled with folk tales that Brewer had collected among older Texas African Americans, many of whom lived, worked, and worshipped in Texas since slavery and reconstruction. With the title "Juneteenth" Dobie published a large group of these folktales in *Tone the Bell Easy*, the 1932 annual journal of the Texas Folklore Society.[12] Brewer became a member of the Society that year, the first African American in the membership. The following year Brewer's second TFS publication, "Old Time Negro Proverbs," appeared in *Spur-of-the-Cock*, also edited by Dobie. Over the next years he published several more articles and collections in the TFS annual journal. One of Brewer's subsequent Texas folklore publications was a collection of stories titled the "John Tales;" they were published in the 1946 TFS publication *Mexican Border Ballads and Other Lore*.[13] That collection is the sixth in our anthology of J. Mason Brewer's writings.

Brewer's fame continued to increase; he became the first black member of the Texas Institute of Letters and the first to hold office in the American Folklore Society. His induction into the Institute of Letters took place in 1953/4. His award-winning *Word on the Brazos* served as the particular publication that led to his Letters membership. Ironically, the ceremony was held at the Driscoll Hotel where Brewer had worked occasionally in earlier years; his entrance and subsequent talk broke segregation at the Driscoll. These honors increased his national prominence that, in addition to the writings from Texas and the Carolinas, derived in part from his well-received collection, *American Negro Folklore*, published by Quadrangle and New York Times Book Company in 1968. Folklore became an important element in the black community in the United States even though they brought few, if any, physical items with them from Africa. As a result, as Brewer noted, "yet though empty handed perforce, they carried in their minds and hearts a treasure of complex musical forms, dramatic speech, and imaginative stories, which they perpetuated through the vital art of self-expression."[14]

John Mason Brewer's area of special interest remained the tales, riddles, jokes, lore, and songs of the African American South, and especially Texas. He collected thousands of these from the reconstruction and post-reconstruction years of the late 19th and early 20th centuries. After *The Word on the Brazos*, Brewer published two more important Texas collections. *Aunt Dicy Tales: Snuff Dipping Tales of the Texas Negro*, was privately published (1956) in Austin in a beautiful limited (400 copies) edition illustrated with original paintings by prominent Texas Southern University artist John T. Biggers and with an "Introduction" by University of Texas scholar, Roy Bedichek. His other major Texas collection, published in 1958, was *Dog Ghosts and Other Texas Negro Folktales*. Dedicated to his mother and his mother-in-law and including drawings from John Biggers and a Foreword by South Carolina scholar Chapman J. Milling, *Dog Ghosts* remains a rich and delightful trove of stories; as Milling pointed out, "even better" than *Word on the Brazos*.[15]

In a review of Brewer's 1953 publication, *The Word on the Brazos*, the *San Francisco Chronicle* writer noted that "J. Mason Brewer can rank with any folklorist." That is an accurate assessment. Brewer regularly made clear the connections of African American folklore with tales and stories from other ethnic groups across the centuries. He noted that African American tales from the Texas Brazos bottoms "followed the pattern of the popular folktale type found in oral literature of other ethnic groups, namely the comic anecdote—a device invented by the masses to lampoon their leaders and superiors."[16] His lifelong commitment to exploring these tales and stories and their varied connections ranked Brewer among the most significant students, collectors, and teachers of folklore in the twentieth century. In fact, Brewer was asked to write the "Introduction" to Henry D. Spalding's *Encyclopedia of Black Folklore and Humor* (1972); the work also included an eighty-page section of Brewer's writings entitled "Plantation to Emancipation." In his brief introduction to Brewer's chapter, Spalding referred to Brewer as "the nation's most illustrious black folklorist."[17]

To Brewer, as to other scholars of African American folklore, the sources and content of the folklore of the black Americans is varied. As Brewer put it, black folk tales have been influenced by their major interests, including religion, work, superstitions, and leisure time activities. Dissimilarities in those and other African American experiences also lead to different types of tales. Brewer distinguishes at least nine different folk tale types: the Preacher tale; the slave tale; black cowboy anecdote; the "Dog Ghost" tale (the dog ghost is a benign, helpful ghost); the snuff-dipping tale; the care-free black man; the Mexican-black anecdote; the Texas Gulf-Coast storm tale; and the animal tale.[18] The latter of course, were particularly prevalent in Old South slave societies and introduced to the nation in the late nineteenth century by Joel Chandler Harris.[19]

We would be short sighted even to think of limiting J. Mason Brewer's contributions only to the study of folklore even though that was his primary field of emphasis. His research, writing, and teaching go well beyond such limits. In addition to his publications from the thirties, *Negrito: Negro Dialect Poems from the Southwest*, *Heralding Dawn: An Anthology of Verse by Texas Negroes*, and *Negro Legislators of Texas: A History of Negroes in Texas Politics from Reconstruction to Disfranchisement*,[20] Brewer published *Patriotic Moments: A Second Book of Verse* (1936); *A History of the Dallas High School for Negroes* (1938); *John Wesley Anderson: A Life in Verse* (1938); *An Historical Outline of the Negro in Travis County* (1940); *More Truth Than Poetry* (1947); and *Silhouettes of Life: A Group of Short Stories* (1948).[21] Brewer's work of verse, his biographical rendition of *John Wesley Anderson*, is the fifth study in our book.

Brewer made use of his time spent at all locales. While in Colorado he wrote materials for an oil company magazine as well as a race-focused periodical. While teaching at Claflin College, he studied black folklore in South Carolina and published *Humorous Folktales of the South Carolina Negro* in 1945. During his time at Livingstone College he published two books, *Three Looks and Some Peeps* (1963) and *Worser Days and Better Times* (1965) as well as two articles, "North Carolina Negro Oral Narratives" and "Animal Tales as Told by African Students of Livingstone College," both published in *North Carolina Folklore*.[22] His prestige continued to increase; the manuscript *Worser Days and Better Times* was published by Chicago-based Quadrangle Books and was exceedingly well-reviewed. It is considered among the best of Brewer's works.

While he resided and worked in Austin during the forties and fifties Brewer became Director of Research as well as Professor of English at Huston-Tillotson. He combined the two interests and positions and strove to encourage students in research, writing, and publication. As a result at least two published works by and with Brewer's students were published, *An Historical Outline of the Negro in Travis County* and *Silhouettes of Life: A Group of Short Stories*. Brewer personally published *More Truth Than Poetry* and *A Pictorial and Historical Souvenir of Negro Life in Austin, Texas, 1950-51*. *More Truth Than Poetry* included illustrations by H. E. Johnson and a copy of Brewer's *Crisis* prize-winning poem, "Bewilderment" on the cover. In the poem, the speaker is unsure how to act when the United States flag goes by, or "America" is sung, because "I know deep down within my soul, my standing is a lie. I'd like to be wholeheartedly devoted to my land. How can I, when blind hatred makes me sit, while others stand?"[23] We have included *More Truth Than Poetry* as the final work of J. Mason Brewer's in our book.

Coinciding with his return to Texas, J. Mason Brewer worked as general editor with John Jenkins and Pemberton Press to publish a series of at least nine previously published works titled "Negro Heritage Series." Among these works were *Memoirs of Elleanore Eldridge; Adventures of an African Slaver, Being a True Account of the Life of Captain Theodore Conot*; and *The Missionary Pioneer: Or a Brief Memoir of the Life, Labors, and Death of John Stewart*.[24] These works are just one more example of the wide range of Brewer's knowledge as well as his commitment to the study and import of African American history and lore.

J. Mason Brewer's last years spent at East Texas State University were busy and productive ones. He was usually listed in the University Catalogue as teaching Literature and Languages. In those years he not only taught classes but, with other faculty, organized symposia and workshops on poetry, folklore, music, and writing. He brought major figures in these areas to the University for discussion and presentation. Of particular value for the students, in addition to Brewer's dynamic instruction, was introducing scholars of African American and Mexican American heritage to campus. Gwendolyn Lawe, currently owner/operator of the A. C. McMillan African American Museum in Emory, Texas, recalls as a student in Brewer's class marveling at his ability to deliver his lectures in verse on occasion.[25]

While at East Texas State University Brewer's interests in folklore turned to major research on the African influence in Mexican folklore. The Brewer Files in the Texas A&M University Commerce Special Collections contain several folders representative of this research which he conducted with Professor Vicente T. Mendoza, a founding member of the Mexican Folklore Society. One sample that Brewer located was an article by an unknown author, "The Tradition of the *Negrito Poeta*."[26] For these efforts, in 1997, the American Folklore Society, meeting in Austin, posthumously granted Brewer the "Companero/a de las Americas" award (UT Austin professor Americo Paredes also received that honor). Unfortunately, according to at least one source, J. Mason Brewer's completed manuscript on the overall topic of African influence on Mexican folklore was destroyed after Brewer's death; whether accidentally or purposely is unclear.

Despite John Mason Brewer's literary life and prestigious career a complete biography of his accomplishments has not been written. Some studies of his life have been completed but they are brief and in two instances, unpublished. Brewer's Texas friend and colleague, East Texas State University professor of English, James W. Byrd, published a short work on Brewer's life in Steck-Vaughn's Southwest Writers

Series. At the time of its publication, Brewer remained at Livingstone College. Two unpublished master's theses have looked at Brewer: Kenneth W. Turner's "Negro Collectors of Negro Folklore: A Study of J. Mason Brewer and Zora Neale Hurston" and Sandra Flowers White's "J. Mason Brewer: An American Folklorist from Texas."[27] Numerous articles have been written about Brewer by authors such as Francis E. Abernethy, James W. Byrd, Bruce A. Glasrud, Lorenzo Thomas, and Darwin T. Turner.[28] Brief bio sketches can be located in the *Handbook of Texas*, *BlackPast Online Encyclopedia*, and *Who's Who in America*. James Byrd published an obituary in the *CLA Journal*.[29] However a book-length biography of this great African American scholar/teacher is still to be written.

Recently, Texas scholar Michael Phillips, evaluated and looked at Brewer's interpretations in two of his publications—*White Metropolis* and "North Texas's Black Art and Literature during the 1920s and 1930s." He found that "themes of intelligence winning over brute force" could be spotted in Brewer's works. Brewer's stories also revealed "a defiant attitude toward white America." Such an emphasis can be noticed in Brewer's poetry such as "Bewilderment," "Deep Ellum," and "NRA" as well as in his folklore and other writings.[30]

While a major study of Brewer's life has been unaddressed his work too has often fallen into obscurity. Many of his publications are almost impossible to locate and others have either been ignored by scholars and readers or remain unknown. For those reasons we chose to put together a collection of the writings of J. Mason Brewer that cover a large portion of his publishing career and that are lesser known or frequently unavailable. John Mason Brewer deserves more recognition. Our book, *J. Mason Brewer, Folklorist and Scholar: His Texas Writings* introduces Brewer's work to the new reader offering a view of the range of the influence and ability of John Mason Brewer. It then is our hope to reclaim and expand recognition for this most significant African American folklore scholar and teacher, and to renew interest in and appreciation for the study and enjoyment of the literature, written and oral, J. Mason Brewer so diligently preserved. Perhaps Lorenzo Thomas, a few years ago, best summarized Brewer's value to us. As Thomas iterated, although Brewer's "*American Negro Folklore* is well known and still much read, there hasn't been much attention devoted to Brewer since his death in 1975. His work, however, was important and remains both delightful and instructive." [31]

—Bruce A. Glasrud and Milton S. Jordan

NOTES

1. "J. Mason Brewer," Texas A&M University Commerce Archives; Michael Barera to Milton S. Jordan, email, August 10, 2015; James W. Byrd, *J. Mason Brewer: Negro Folklorist* (Austin: Steck Vaughn, 1967), 4. East Texas State University had been the last state supported university to integrate the student body when it allowed black students to enroll in the summer of 1964.

2. Brewer Files, Special Collections Library, TAMUC; Dedication to *Word on the Brazos: Negro Preacher Tales from the Brazos Bottoms of Texas* (Austin: University of Texas Press, 1953).

3. "J. Mason Brewer," Texas A&M University Commerce Archives; Brewer Files, Special Collections Library, TAMUC; "A Negro Cowboy: J. H. Brewer," in *American Negro Folklore*, edited by J. Mason Brewer (New York: New York Times Books, 1968), 275-278.

4. Byrd, *J. Mason Brewer*, 3-4; Brewer Files, TAMUC.

5. Byrd, *J. Mason Brewer*, 3-4; Brewer Files, TAMUC; J. Mason Brewer, *Echoes of Thought* (Fort Worth: Progressive Printing Company, 1922); ; J. Mason Brewer, *Glimpses of Life* (Fort Worth: Progressive Printing Company, 1923).

6. Byrd, *J. Mason Brewer*, 4; Bruce A. Glasrud, "John Mason Brewer," *BlackPast Online Encyclopedia* (http://www.blackpast.org).

7. John Mason Brewer, ed., *Patriotic Moments; A Second Book of Verse* (Dallas: privately printed, 1936); John Mason Brewer, ed., *A History of the Dallas High School for Negroes* (1938; Dallas: Friends of the Dallas Public Library, 1991).

8. Byrd, *J. Mason Brewer*, 4; Glasrud, "John Mason Brewer," *BlackPast Online*; Sandra F. White, "J. Mason Brewer: An African American Folklorist from Texas" (Master's thesis, University of Houston, Clear lake, 1997), 17.

9. J. Mason Brewer, *Negrito: Negro Dialect Poems of the Southwest* (San Antonio: Naylor, 1933); J. Mason Brewer, *The Negro in Texas History* (Dallas: Mathis Publishing, 1936); J. Mason Brewer, ed., *Heralding Dawn: An Anthology of Verse by Texas Negroes* (Dallas: June Thomason Printing, 1936); J. Mason Brewer, *Negro Legislators of Texas and Their Descendants: A History of the Negro in Texas Politics from Reconstruction to Disfranchisement* (Dallas: Mathis Publishing, 1935).

10. Lorraine Barnes, "J. Mason Brewer," in *A Pictorial and Historical Souvenir of Negro Life in Austin, Texas, 1950-5* (Austin: privately printed, 1951), 2; Byrd, *J. Mason Brewer*, 4; Glasrud, "John Mason Brewer," *BlackPast Online*; White, "J. Mason Brewer," 17-18. White and Byrd pointed out that Brewer earned his master's degree from Indiana University in 1933.

11. J. Mason Brewer, *The Word on the Brazos: Negro Preacher Tales from the Brazos Bottoms of Texas* (Austin: University of Texas Press, 1953).

12. Byrd, *J. Mason Brewer*, 4; White, "J. Mason Brewer," 17-18; J. Mason Brewer, "Juneteenth," *Tone the Bell Easy*, edited by J. Frank Dobie (Austin: Texas Folklore Society, 1932), 9-54.

13. John Mason Brewer, "Old Time Negro Proverbs." *Spur-of-the-Cock*, edited by J. Frank Dobie (Austin: Texas Folklore Society, 1933), 101-105; J. Mason Brewer, "John Tales," *Mexican Border Ballads and other Lore*, edited by Modie C. Boatright (Austin: Texas Folklore Society, 1946), 81-104.

14. Brewer, *Word On the Brazos*; Byrd, *J. Mason Brewer*, 4-5; White, "J. Mason Brewer," 17, 20, 23; J. Mason Brewer, *American Negro Folklore* (New York: Quadrangle/New York Times Book Company, 1968).

15. J. Mason Brewer, *Aunt Dicy Tales: Snuff-Dipping Tales of the Texas Negro* (Austin: privately printed, 1956); J. Mason Brewer, *Dog Ghosts and Other Texas Negro Folk Tales* (Austin: University of Texas Press, 1958), Milling comment on p. xiv.

16. *San Francisco Chronicle*, cited in Byrd, *J. Mason Brewer*, p. 15; Brewer, *The Word on the Brazos*, quote on p. 13.

17. Henry D. Spalding, ed., *Encyclopedia of Black Folklore and Humor* (New York: Jonathan David Publishers, 1972), quote on p. 71; Brewer, "Introduction," in Spalding, *Encyclopedia*, pp. ix-x; Brewer, "Plantation to Emancipation," in Spalding, *Encyclopedia*, 71-157.

18. J. Mason Brewer, "Texas Negro Tales," *Interracial Review* (December 1959), 236-237.

19. On Joel Chandler Harris, see J. Mason Brewer's sister's excellent study, Stella Brewer Brookes, *Joel Chandler Harris—Folklorist* (Athens: University of Georgia Press, 1950).

20. Brewer, *Negrito*; Brewer, *Heralding Dawn*; Brewer, *Negro Legislators of Texas*.

21. Brewer, ed., *Patriotic Moments;* Brewer, ed., *A History of the Dallas High School for Negroes;* John Mason Brewer, *John Wesley Anderson: A Life in Verse* (Dallas: Clyde C. Cockrell & Sons, 1938); John Mason Brewer, *An Historical Outline of the Negro in Travis County* (Austin: Samuel Huston College, 1940); John Mason Brewer, *More Truth Than Poetry* (Austin: privately printed, 1947); John Mason Brewer, ed., *Silhouettes of Life: A Group of Short Stories* (Austin: Samuel Huston College, 1948).

22. John Mason Brewer, *Humorous Folktales of the South Carolina Negro* (Orangeburg, SC: Claflin College Press, 1945); John Mason Brewer, *Three Looks and Some Peeps* (Salisbury, NC: privately printed, 1963); John Mason Brewer, *Worser Days and Better Times* (Chicago: Quadrangle Books, 1965). John Mason Brewer, "Animal Tales as Told by African Students of Livingstone College," *North Carolina Folklore* 16 (May 1968); John Mason Brewer, "North Carolina Negro Oral Narratives," *North Carolina Folklore* 9 (July 1961), 21-33.

23. J. Mason Brewer, ed., *An Historical Outline of the Negro in Travis County* (Austin: Samuel Huston College, 1940); J. Mason Brewer, ed., *Silhouettes of Life: A Group of Short Stories*

(Austin: Samuel Huston College, 1948); J. Mason Brewer, *More Truth Than Poetry* (Austin: privately printed, 1947); and J. Mason Brewer, *A Pictorial and Historical Souvenir of Negro Life in Austin, Texas, 1950-51* (Austin: privately printed, 1951). "Bewilderment" quote from cover, *More Truth Than Poetry*.

24. J. Mason Brewer, ed. *Memoirs of Elleanore Eldridge* (Austin: Pemberton Press, 1969); J. Mason Brewer, ed., *Adventures of an African Slaver, Being a True Account of the Life of Captain Theodore Conot* (Austin: Pemberton Press, 1969); J. Mason Brewer, ed., *The Missionary Pioneer: Or a Brief Memoir of the Life, Labors, and Death of John Stewart* (Austin: Pemberton Press, 1969).

25. Gwendolyn Lawe, conversation with Bruce Glasrud, February 20, 2016.

26. John Mason Brewer, "The Tradition of the *Negrito Poeta*," Brewer Files, Texas A&M University Commerce, Special Collections.

27. Byrd, *J. Mason Brewer;* Kenneth W. Turner, "Negro Collectors of Negro Folklore: A Study of J. Mason Brewer and Zora Neale Hurston" (Master's thesis, East Texas State University, 1964); White, "J. Mason Brewer: An American Folklorist from Texas."

28. Francis E. Abernethy, "African-American Folklore in Texas and in the Texas Folklore Society," in *Juneteenth Texas: Essays in African-American Folklore*, edited by Francis E. Abernethy, Patrick B. Mullen, and Alan B. Govenar (Denton, Texas: University of North Texas Press, 1996), 1-13; James W. Byrd, "Dr. J. Mason Brewer," in *Features and Fillers: Texas Journalists on Texas Folklore*, edited by Jim Harris (Denton: University of North Texas Press, 1999), 168-171; Bruce A. Glasrud, "From Griggs to Brewer: A Review of Black Texas Culture, 1899-1940," *Journal of Big Bend Studies* 15 (2003), 195-212; Lorenzo Thomas, "The African-American Folktale and J. Mason Brewer," in *Juneteenth Texas: Essays in African-American Folklore*, edited by Francis E. Abernethy, Patrick B. Mullen,

and Alan B. Govenar (Denton, Texas: University of North Texas Press, 1996), 222-235; Darwin T. Turner "J. Mason Brewer: Vignettes," *CLA Journal* 18 (June 1975), 570-577.

29. James W. Byrd, "John Mason Brewer." *The Handbook of Texas Online* (http://www.tshaonline.org/handbook/online); Bruce A. Glasrud, "John Mason Brewer," *BlackPast Online Encyclopedia* (http://www.blackpast.org); *Who's Who in America* (1975); James W. Byrd, "In Memory of John Mason Brewer (1896-1975)," *CLA Journal* 18 (June 1975), 578-81.

30. Michael Phillips, *White Metropolis* (Austin: University of Texas Press, 2006), 108; Michael Phillips, "North Texas's Black Art and Literature," in *The Harlem Renaissance in the American West*, edited by Bruce A. Glasrud and Cary D. Wintz (New York: Routledge, 2012), 29-31, quotes on 29.

31. Thomas, "The African-American Folktale and J. Mason Brewer," in *Juneteenth Texas*, 222-235 231.

--ONE--
ME AND JIM MYERS

The following story was told by John Mason Brewer's father, J. H. Brewer, to J. Mason Brewer who proceeded to write it down. His father not only worked as a cowhand, as portrayed in this story, but also in numerous related jobs in the latter nineteenth and early twentieth centuries. The late J. H. Brewer eventually became a barber; until he died on May 26, 1961, at the age of ninety-two, he was still barbering with a steady hand.

This source was located in the Archives of Texas A&M University Commerce. Mason Brewer wrote and then carefully edited the document, "Me and Jim Myers." Reprinted by permission.

***

When I was eighteen years old I was awful little and real skinny and kind of sickly, so a Goliad doctor told me I would have to work out in the open as much as possible if I wanted to be healthy and strong. He advised me to get work on a ranch and become a cowhand.

Luckily it was not hard to follow his advice, because Mama did day work in town sometimes for a ranch owner by the name of Dillard Fant. Colonel Fant and his family thought a whole lot of Mama, so when she asked him to give me a job as a cowhand on one of his ranches he said "All right, Martha (that was Mama's name), I'll give the boy a job if you want him to have it." So Colonel Fant loaded me on a wagon one Saturday morning with some more Goliad men he had hired as cowhands and carried me out to one of his ranches. The name of the ranch was the Santa Rosa, or Media-Luna (Halfmoon) Ranch, and it was located about fifty miles north of the Rio Grande River and twenty-five miles on the other side of the King

Ranch. Part of it was in Hidalgo County, and part of it was in Cameron County.

Colonel Fant had a contract with the government to furnish beef for the Indians in the Indian Territory, so he employed about a hundred Negroes and Mexicans to drive his herds up the trail every year or work the cattle he sold and shipped by train to Ardmore, Oklahoma.

The year I started working for Colonel Fant was 1887, and I didn't get very far up the trail that first trip. We had barely got started; the fact of it is we hardly reached Live Oak County when our whole herd was sold to another ranch owner by the name of George West. So instead of using our crew to drive cattle up the trail that year, Colonel Fant had us to build a water tank on one of his ranches in Live Oak County. We started building the tank in April and finished it on August 12, but a cyclone came along on August 13, and it was blown to pieces – over a hundred days of hard work by twenty-five men wrecked in just a few minutes.

But it was the year 1888 that I remember most, because that was my first year to really go all the way up the trail. The reason I remember my first full trip up the trail so well is because of some trouble I had with a trail boss named Jim Myers. Jim was about thirty years old, five feet and seven inches tall, and so light in complexion he could have passed for white. But he was an ill-tempered and overbearing man. Colonel Fant had made me second trail boss and Jim first trail boss. The Colonel said that the reason he made me second trail boss was that I had a level head and knew better how to get along with the other cowhands than Jim did. Jim didn't say nothing to Colonel Fant before we left the Media-Luna, but I could tell by the way he acted and the look on his face when he looked at me after we got started up the trail that he didn't like it about Colonel Fant making me second trail boss.

I didn't see much of Jim because, as I'm sure you already know, the duty of a trail boss was to ride ahead and find a suitable bedding place for the cattle sleeping area every night and to locate water where the herds could drink. So Jim spent very little time with the herd and the rest of the crew. But whenever he was with us he would look at me in a way that I knew meant trouble ahead. I didn't know in what form the trouble was gonna come, but I kept my eyes on Jim whenever he was around and watched his every move.

The trouble came one morning after we had been on the trail about five weeks – about the first week in May 1888. It usually took about three months to reach Colonel Fant's headquarters ranch in the Indian Territory, and we had started driving the herd up the trail about the last week in March, so we were about halfway to the headquarters ranch when me and Jim had it out. The way it happened was like this: The camp cook was having calf steaks for breakfast that morning, an occasion that was always looked forward to with great pleasure by the cowhands because it wasn't often that a calf was killed and they had an opportunity to enjoy this trail driver's delicacy.

We were all seated around on the ground in a circle when Jim drove up, got down off of his horse, and took a seat among us. I was just taking a nice, juicy calf steak out of the pan with my fork when Jim sat down. As soon as he sat down he looked at me with an angry scowl on his face and said, "John, git up out of that pan and pass that pan of meat over here to me."

"Git up out of that pan of meat?" I said, glaring back at him. "I knew I was small, but I didn't know I was little enough to git in a pan. And now, do you want this meat?" So I took my foot and kicked the pan over to where Jim was sitting, and when I did this he jumped to his feet, pointed his finger in my face, and yelled, "What's the matter with you, John? Do you think I'm a dog?"

"I don't know, but you sho do act like one," I replied. And when I said this Jim yelled, "I've had enough of this!" and started for his gun. But when he started for it I put my hand on my gun right quick and said, "If you put your hands on that gun, Jim, I'll kill you." This took Jim by surprise because he had borrowed what he thought was my only pistol about three weeks before, and he had no idea that I had another gun. So looking at me he said, "Where'd you git that gun? I thought you loaned me the only gun you had."

"Yeah, I know that's what you thought," I replied, "but I had two instead of one."

"Well, what's the matter with you?" Jim continued.

"Nothing," I replied in return. "Something's wrong with you." He never said any more, so I finished eating my calf steak and got on my horse and rode out to where the cattle were grazing and told Bill McKenzie, one of the cowhands who had been watching the cattle all night, to ride into camp and get his breakfast – that I'd relieve him. So Bill got on his horse and rode into camp for his breakfast like I told him to do. But when Bill rode into camp and sat down and started eating, Jim jumped up and said, "Who told you to leave that herd and come in here and eat?" All the cowhands called me "the little one" because I was the smallest as well as the youngest man in the crew, so Bill looked up at Jim and said, "The little one told me to come in an' get my breakfast 'cause we have to make a big drive today an' oughta get started early."

"The little one ain't got no right to tell you to do nothin'," said Jim. "Now you go right back on out there and start watching them cattle again like you was doin'."

"I ain't gonna do no such a thing," said Bill, rising to his feet an' drawing his pistol on Jim. "The little one told me to come in here an' git my breakfast an' that's what I'm gonna do. You don't know how to treat a man nohow; if it hadn't been for the little one we would of all quit the trail weeks ago when you acted a fool with us. The little one got us to stay on, an' we gonna do what he says do."

When Bill said this, Jim jumped on his horse and rode out where I was watching the herd and said "John, what's the matter with you?" I still had my hand on my pistol, so I said, "Nothin', Jim; there must be something wrong with you." So he said, "Well, I reckon it is me, John. I have to deal with so much confusion, riding ahead by myself all day without anybody to talk to, so I reckon I am a little quick on the trigger when it comes to gittin' mad, so let's shake hands and furgit it." So I told Jim that was all right with me and we shook hands and didn't have no more trouble all the way to Fort Supply.

After we delivered the cattle I never saw Jim no more. Reports had it that he married a German girl, bought him a farm in the Indian Territory, and settled down and raised a family.

The other cowhands went on back to the Media-Luna, but I stayed on so I could come back on the train with the horses. The train that I came back on had one car full of barrels of whiskey being shipped into Texas and had a wreck after we started off. Some Indians came and took away the broken barrels of whiskey and got drunk. I drank some of the whiskey, too, but didn't get drunk. About a week later I was back on the Santa Rosa ranch getting ready for another trail drive. One thing more I forgot to tell you was about the horse races they always had at Fort Supply every July Fourth. The horse races were one of the main attractions of the day. They always had four horses in the races – an army horse, a civilian horse, an Indian horse, and a cowboy horse.

The same year that me and Jim Myers had that trouble I was selected to ride the cowboy horse in the race because I was light in weight and jockey size. We got started when the gun went off, and I was in the lead until we got within fifty yards of the finishing line. Then all of a sudden the Indian who was right in behind me let out a whoop, threw his hands up in the air, and his horse shot past me like a streak of lightning. Of course he won the race.

—J. H. Brewer

--TWO--
GLIMPSES OF LIFE: POEMS

Early in his professional career, while teaching and serving as an elementary school principal in Fort Worth, John Mason Brewer published two books of poetry; each was published by the Progressive Printing Company. The first was published in 1922 and was titled *Echoes of Thought*; the second, *Glimpses of Life*, was published the following year, 1923. It included a Preface written by K. W. McMillan, pastor at St. Andrews M.E. Church. The short book was divided into two sections, one called Dialect and the other Depth. Dialect was comprised of twelve poems and Depth twenty. On the title page was a poem that depicted "glimpses of life." It follows:

> The drip, drip, drip of a rainy day
> That wearies the soul and mind;
> A chanting bird with his springtime lay
> That keeps one feeling fine;
> A twilight sun that tints the sky
> With a rose enchanted hue;
> The song of a brook that's gurgling
> Beneath a cloudless blue.

Originally published as John Mason Brewer, *Glimpses of Life: Poems* (Fort Worth: Progressive Printing Co., 1923). Reprinted with permission.

***

PREFACE

The poems which are comprised in this book are written by Prof. J. Mason Brewer, who is now Principal of the Rosen Heights Elementary public school of Fort Worth, Texas.

They were published in this form because they have attracted attention for their grasp of facts, philosophical breadth, and clear generalization. Their intrinsic value and merit for the people who have read them is hereby attested.

This is the second published edition from the pen of Prof. Brewer. If you have read his *Echoes of Thought*, I am sure you have been charmed by the language, thought, and diction.

In the present work the author has directed his chief attention to the human life as seen and studied by the Negro, giving a true story in poetry of their relation to each other. Both the forms themselves and their changes are traceable only in the facts and history of the race. So in presenting this book, he presents not a recital, but an interpretation of life.

It is the purpose of the author to inspire and spur the perplexed youth of his race to act Columbus to his own undiscovered possibilities, to urge him not to brood over the past, nor dream of the future, but to get his lesson from the hour; to encourage him to make every occasion a great occasion, for he cannot tell when the fate may take his measure for a higher place; to show him that he must not wait for his opportunity, but make it.

If this volume shall open wider the door of some narrow life and awaken powers before unknown, the author will feel repaid for his labor.

The writer of this book is a College Graduate of Wiley University, and has taught in the Public Schools of Austin and Fort Worth since his graduation. He is Superintendent of the Sunday School of St. Andrew's Methodist Episcopal Church of Fort Worth and may well fit into the program of any community that has for its object, thrift, high and better living.

–K. W. McMillan
Pastor St. Andrew's M. E. Church

DIALECT

Brother Brown's Logic

Since de world had its beginnin'
It's been changin' all erlong;
Fo'ks an' nations has been sinnin'
An' been stannin' up fo' wrong;
Dis hyeah ain't so pow'ful funny,
Case a pusson's prone to err;
But whene'er de church begs money,
Dat's a little bit too fer.

I knows, too, de world is movin'
An' dat t'ings has changed uh heap;
But wid all dis hyeah improvin'
What we sows is what we reap;
So de shepherd who lubs Jesus
Is mos' sartin to succeed;
What he says is gonna please us,
An' we'll nebber be in need.

On de udder han', de pusson
Who bas allus got uh bill;
So de church can git a cussin'
'Bout some do' uh window sill--
Ain't de parson uh mah likin'
Ef he's built a church ob gol',
'Case de members's allus strikin',
 An' we'se allus in de hole.

Now mah logic may be branded
As de sayin's ob uh fool;
An' I may be rep'imanded
By de fo'ks whose been to school;
But I lubs mah church an' marster,

'Case dey found me when I'se lost;
I ain't servin' jes de pastor,
But de savior ob de cross.

When We Go To Milk the Cow

When we go to milk de cow
We mos' allus has uh row;
Sook she sta't to switch her tail
Lef' an' right, an' in de pail,
Dis make pa as mad as fiah;
Sez he to her, "Now, look hyeah;
What'd ab tell you 'bout dat deed'?
I'se gwine tak' away yo' feed."

Sook she look an' raise ber hoof;
Sends de milk pail to de roof;
Pa he says, "Heuh, hol' dis pan;
On her back I'se gona lan'."

So he chase her roun' an' roun';
On his face an orful frown;
Sook she run an' jump an' kick
Evah time she gits uh lick.

Pa at las' begins to sweat;
Sook gits tiahed an' stahts to fret;
Pa uh hittin' on her back;
She uh moanin' at each whack.

After dis Sook acts alright;
Pa he sez dat cow's uh sight;
Sez if milk wuz sellin' low,
Dat he'd Jet de rascal go.

The Egotist

I jes com' f'om down mah gal's house;
B'lieve me she's uh teasin' brown;
I don' know jes what 'ud happen
Ef she'd try to put me down;
I don't tink she'll eber drap me
Cae mah hair is good an' slick;
So I jes can't see no reason
Why mah Lucy ougbta kick.

I got little feet an' hans too;
Keeps mah finger nails in prime;
Spends mah ha'fs an' all mah quatahs
Givin' her uh plum good time;
Now de suits I war' is classy;
Fits me lak uh fashion plate;
I keeps up wid all de changes;
I ain't nebber out ob date;

Shines mah shoes mos' ebry hour;
Changes collars ebry day;
Now you know 'taint many youngsters
Dat takes care deyse'f dat way;
I'se got silks ob all descriptions
F'om mah shirts down to mah sox;
I has ties ob all de patterns;
I has got 'em by de box.

Now de job I has it pays me,
So I has a bank account;
I can write a check at leisure
Jes almos' fo' any 'mount;
I'm some classy an' I know it;
She don't haf' to tell me so;
Case she knows dey ain't nobody
Dat can come up to her beau.

Sister Susan's Complaint

I'se o' pillar ob dis structure,
An' bas been dese many years;
Here I'se smiled an' laffed o' plenty
An' I'se also shed some tears;
Den I t'inks I has uh right, sah,
Fo' to 'spress mah soul's desiah,
So how come dey had dat fiddle
Up dere Sunday in de choir?

Now I'se been hyeah fo' o' long time,
An' de singin's been jes fin';
Ev'ry Sunday dey's been singin',
An' it sho' has eased mah min';
But las' Sunday when dat fiddle
Butted in an' change de soun',
Ev'rybody in de service
Sit back in deir seats an' frown.

Now I wants to know de reason
Why dey brung dat fiddle dere,
An' jes who it wuz who's playin'
Wid dat slicked up, greasy hair;
Actin's if he owned de buildin'
An' de members, too, I guess;
How disgustin' he wuz lookin'
I can't fin' woids to express.

Why, dat fiddle soun' so funny,
Till nobody did'ent shout;
So I com' down here to see, sah
Jes what dis wuz all erbout;
I don' believe in bringin' Satan
Into churches any time,
So I hopes dat you'll remove it
So we'll reach dat heabenly clime.

Go On, Chile, Go On!

Y'oughta seen me Sat'day night;
I wuz so' 'nuff lookin' right;
Had mah bes' outfit all on;
Sittin' down upon her lawn;
    Go on, chile, go on!

Sorter touched her li'l han';
Said she lak'ed it sumthin gran;
Gazed into dem lovin' eyes,
Felt mah hea't beat kind'a wise;
    Go on, chile, go on!

I begin to whisper low
Dat I lubbed her, lubbed her so
She begin to kind'a smile
Wid her manna's an' her style;
    Go on, chile, go on!

Now an' den I heah her sigh
As she gaze up in de sky;
Den Ah looks at ol' man moon,
An' Ah hums uh li'l tune;
    Go on, chile, go on!

Had a question in mah min',
But de words wuz hard to fin';
Ah know'd what I oughta as';
But wuz slow about de yas';
    Go on, chile, go on!

Ise de proudes' man in town
'Case she nebber turned me down;
So I'se gwine'a hab uh mate,
'Case we bof' done set de date;
    Go on, chile, go on!

His Preference

You kin talk about yo' Cad'lacs an' yo' Hudsons superfine;
You can mention how dey engines an' dey motors allus shine;
You can speak about de body, an' de beauty ob its frame,
But me an' mah ol' tin lizzie has you bested jes de same.

She will take me to de city, ef it's rainin' uh it's dry;
'Tain't a mudhole dat will stall her, 'case her motto's do uh die;
You can treat her lak you want'a, makes no diffunce what youse done;
Wid a piece ob wire or kindlin' you can fix her so she'll run.

Now, dere's lots a cars dut's bigger, an' dat costs uh hol' lot mo',
But dere ain't uh car dats better, be it six uh be it four;
'Case de li'l f livver knows me, an' she knows I know her, too;
So wid dis hyeah understandin', we mos' allus makes it thoo.

When de othah cars is puffin', tryin' to pull some big, steep hill,
Mah tin lizzie sails on by 'em, an' dey wondahs at her skill;
Othah fo'ks can hab dey Marmons, an' dey Lincolns ef dev mus',
But de good ole car dat Henry made is good enuf fo' us.

A Conclusion

When you visits a convention,
Or a Conference, eider one;
Dey's so filled up wid dissension
Till dey ain't no bizness done;
Dey jes squabbles, an' goes yellin'
'Bout de ones whose in de lead,
Sayin' dat it's lies dey's tellin',
Dat dere ain't no such a creed.

Seems to me dey ain't no sperit
When dese brethren takes de flo';
Ebry time one speaks dey jeer it
An' say we don' wan' no mo';
Dis hyeah preacher he's uh 'spirin'
Fo' a job dat pays 'im high,
An' annuder he's a wirin'
Fo' some dough to git 'im by.

Ef a feller's church is little,
He ain't recok'nized a'tall;
He jes plays de secon' fiddle,
An' dey rolls 'im lak uh ball;
When at las' de meetin's ended
An' de trip back home's begun,
You can say dat youse attended,
But you can't show what youse done.

When Mah Wesley Plays

Seems de day am bright an' fair,
An' dere's fragrance in de air;
Ain't uh sad tho't comes erroun',
Nebber is one single frown,
      When mah Wesley plays.

'Pears dat all de earth am gay,
An' de clouds don' com' no mo';
Seems ah hears de breezes say,
 "Ain't she got de gran'nes beau'!"
      When mah Wesley plays.

Watermelons on de vine,
Seems to tingle in dey veins;
When he plays dat baby mine,
What am sweet as dat dar strain
      When mah Wesley plays.

Earth an' sky too seems to stop,
An' be listenin' to de tune
Dat am bein' played so prop'
By a man dat's called uh coon,
      When mah Wesley plays.

Animals erroun' all gathahs
Fo' to heah him pluck de keys;
All de fowls wid deir fethahs
Sits erroun' an' seems well pleased
      When mah Wesley plays.

All de flowers an' de grass
Seems to sway wid ebr'y song;
An' de neighbo's as dey pass
Has to stop an' lingah long
      When mah Wesley plays.

Ef I'se angry when he calls
An' attempts to sulk fo' fun;
When he sta'ts to play I falls
An' begins to call him 'hon,"
      When mah Wesley plays.

You can talk about yo Moza'ts
An' yo' Beethovens an' sich;
But de' music touches heap mo' hea'ts
F'om de po'es to de rich
      When mah Wesley plays.

Dat Radio

Ef you sends John to de city
Fo' to pay uh bill or so;
An' it takes 'im nin'ey minutes,
'Taint no need fo' you to blow;
Jes go on an' take it quiet'y,
'Case de world am on de go;
An' yo' John am movin' wid it,
'Case he lubs de radio.

Ef you visits at yo' neighbo's
An' dey acts a li'l queer,
Don' git angry wid 'em, honey,
Dey jes wants to try to heah;
Dey jes wants to heah de band play,
An' dey's glad dat it's fixed so
Dey can stay at home an' hyeah it,
'Case dey got uh radio.

Ef you goes down to de drugsto'
An' you can't git waited on;
But you sees uh crowd a star'in
'Roun' uh great big wide mouf horn;
You jes mought as well be seated,
'Case dey ain't gwine wuk' no mo'
Till de big concert am ended
On dat bloomin' radio.

When we sta'ted makin' street cars,
I 'tought we wuz goin' fas';
An' I sho' did t'ink we'se sailin'
When de auto come to pass;
Den dey went an' mak' de airplane
'Case de auto wuz too slow;
But dey sho' did cap de climax
When dey found dis radio.

A Lesson in Family Pride

Come hyeah, honey, let yo' mammy
Tell you sumthin 'bout yo' pa;
What he done when he's uh Sammy,
An' uh fightin' in de war;
You don't know, I hardly reckon,
Dat yo' daddy crossed de sea
Wid de good o' nine'y secon'
Fo' de sake o' liberty.

When de country wuz a-callin'
Fo' some men to volunteer,
An' de shot an' shell wuz fallin',
I jes' couldent keep 'im here;
He enlisted in the ahmy
Fo' to whop de brutish Hun;
An' when things 'ud git real stormy
He wuz right dar with his gun.

He dident git behin' de otbahs
When de smoke wuz thick an' black;
But he'd stan' up wid his brothahs
An' he'p send dem Germans back;
He wuz allus good an' ready
When he heerd de firin' call;
An' he'd aim so true an' steady,
Till dey couldn't he'p but fall.

In de thickes' ob de battle,
When de shot an' shell would burst;
An' you'd heah de mighty rattle
Ob de conflict at its worse;
You could hyeah yo' pa uh singin'
Ev'ry time he'd wing uh Hun;
An' fo' long de news wuz ringin'
Dat de U.S.A. had won.

The Migrant

I has heerd about de freedom up above de Dixon line;
Fo' de longes' I'se been seekin' peace, an' res' fo' dis ol' min'
So at las' I'se' found a haben whar de people's min's is high,
An' you'se rated by yo' larnin', 'taint de grin dat gits you by.

Sixty year has been, I reckon, since Abe Lincoln sot us free,
An' de news spread thru de country, dat we had ouah liberty;
But de freedom dat wuz gin' us wuz a camou-flagin' kin',
An' I'se nebber had real freedom, 'till I got above dat line.

'Fore I lef' de southland's borders, dis ol' frame wuz givin' down,
An' de smile I'se use to
wearin' had done turned
into a frown;
But today de ol' frame's stronger, gittin' long de fines' kin',
An' I'se smilin' more than eber, 'case I'se up above dat line.

Use to hang mah haid in sorrow, 'case dey graded
us as low,
An' dey made us tink we'se nuthin, 'case we didn't
hab no show;
But I hol's mah haid up higher, an' I'se lifted up in min',

An' I feels lak' I'se a human, since I'se been above dat line.
I don't heah no pow'ful speeches 'bout de ol' black mammy's place,
How she nussed ol' massa's chillun, an' conceded fo' de race;
But I heahs de leaders speakin' 'bout de smartness ob' ouah kin',
An' de way ouah fo'ks is risin' up above de Dixon line.

I has caught a broadah vision ob de country's good, I 'clare,
An' I'se found out dat it really tries to stan' fo' what is fair,
Fo' dey puts dey foot on merit, dat's de only way you'll shine;
Dere's a secon' proclamation, up above de Dixon line.

DEPTH

When Morn Doth Wake

When morn doth wake, the struggle then begins
Between the selves, and lasts until day ends;
Ye would do good if nature had its way
But yet it seems some base instinct holds sway;
The battle grim continues all the while;
We know not which shall conquer-frown or smile;
For pain or joy, we know not which shall be
When morn doth wake throughout eternity.

When morn doth wake, what shadows hover nigh!
We know not which 'twill be, to laugh or cry;
The conflict bold between the worst and best
Goes on for aye; it is an endless test;
The heart-throbs true which you desire to feel
May bring to you a littlewoe, or weal;
You cannot tell which way the tide will turn--
When morn doth wake, your soul may soar or burn.

When morn doth wake, what beauty shall we see?
We know not what the hours to come will be;
They may be glad, they could be otherwise;
Sometimes a tear, perhaps a sweet surprise;
What pangs, and pains of sorrow may appear;
What things occur that bring to us good cheer;
Shall passion gay or purity mean more
When morn doth wake upon that other shore.

Love's Definition

Love carries with it devotion
To whatever is right, and good;
It's not only expression, but motion
Imbibed in the soul of manhood.

My Fountains

At the top of the peak of life there lies
Two fountains that bubble beneath blue skies;
Reflecting sincerity as hey flow,
And water that causes my soul to grow.
And ever as I gaze :md think,
And with my eyes their beauty drink,
All burdens that appear pass on;
My fountains rare proclaim the dawn.

When hope and charity both fail,
And every songbird quits his rail;
I look into my founts and see
A glimmer of fidelity.

When heart and mind are sorely tried,
And all the world seems cursed with pride
I gaze up at my founts and feel
A sympathetic touch that's real.
Whene'r the muse on wings does fly
To lands where I can't hear her cry; I
look into my founts and yearn,
And instantly she will return.

When toil at length brings no
reward, And from success it seems
I'm barred;
I gaze up at my founts, and see
Success in all its verity.

Some Day

I know, although the way seems dark,
And heart and mind are burdened, too;
Some day, fair dame, you'll make your mark;
Some others have, and why not you
        As well as they?
I think the trials that you hear
From early morn till setting sun;
And all the things which are unfair
That people specify you've done
        Will cease some day.

What matters it if sorrow comes
With all its pangs and woes?
Let gladness and thyself be chums
And revel in her throes
        With heart that's gay!
Some day the clouds above will part
And sunshine gay peep down;
Injecting into thy pure heart
Rays, which with joy abound
        In every way.

Smile when adverses reach your side;
Be calm when there's a changing tide;
Be steadfast, true, thou musy wsucceed;
A damsel fair, a flower, no weed
        Which will decay.
Heed not the sneering of the crowd,
Although embarrassment it brings;
Some day they nurtured aim, endowed
With purer, higher, nobler things,
        Will have its day.

A Prayer

Ah, Master, may I walk, and talk with thee for just a little while;
I need thy loving, tender care to make that other mile;
There is no human hand that leads one to the goal he's set;
Thou in thy goodness, and thy grace has healing balm to let.
I tremble, lest I falter and forget, thy guiding hand will lead;
But in a flash my mind reflects, thou art my friend indeed;
Teach me from no other
source true solace to
expect,
But know, down in my soul of
souls, that thou alone art all
correct.

'Tis Night

Sunbeam have ceased to wander,
The last sun ray has fled;
Bright stars appear out yonder,
Their silver light thy shed;
But as bright as they are shining
Their glitter seems but faint;
Brings naught to me but pining; 'Tis
night, I feel its taint.

Love dreams enthrall no longer,
Heart throbs beat false, not true;
Unfaithfulness beats stronger
Its doleful, sad tattoo;
Contentment has been stifled;
Of longing there's none such;
Fond mem'ries have been rifled;
'Tis night, I feel its touch.

Unless

I care not for the flowers
Unless they love bestow;
Or brighten someone's hours
Whose heart doth nourish woe.

I care not for the singing
Of little birds so gay,
Unless their songs are bringing
Hope, to some life's dark day.

I care not for the sunlight Which
bathes the verdant hills
Unless by virtue of its sight
It cures some human ills.

I care not for the beauty
Of human form or face,
Unless it wake to duty
Some soul unsaved by grace.

The Pharisee and the Publican

The Pharisee thought not of others,
His accomplishments stayed on his mind;
He cared just for self, but his his brothers
No care for their wants did he find;
His desire was to boast, not to humble
Himself, and unselfishly pray;
So, since his desire was to grumble,
He kept the dear saviour away.

The Publican thought of the Master,
And begged Him have mercy, for he
Said, "I am not worthy, oh, Master,
To bow in submission to thee."
He came in a spirit of wanting
To be helped, by the savior of men;
And because he himself was not wanting
He made of the saviour a friend.

If You Understood Me, and I Understood You

If you understood me, and I understood you,
As we plod up the hill of life;
Then each fellow would know what the other
would do;
There'd be no ill-feeling, or strife;
For I'd know your habits, and you would
know mine.
And all of the things we would say
Would be taken by each one as words
that were kind,
For we'd both know the other's way.

If you understood me, and I understood you,
You never would think I was mean,
And I'd change all the bad thoughts I had
about you,
And our minds would be pretty clean;
I would stop thinking then, that you thought you
were grand,
And puffed up with self and conceit;
You would think then that I was the right sort
of man,
That a fellow would like to meet.

If you understood me, and I understood you,
I would say what I thought was right,
And I could not be changed then, by no gang or
crew,
Because I was out of your sight;
And you'd always be frank in your dealings
with me,
For you'd know how much I could pack;
You would say to my face what you
thought about me,

And stick to it behind my back.

If you understood me, and I understood you.
I'd he'p you to carry your load;
I would never have something I wanted to do,
If you had broke down in the road;
And whate'er you possessed you would willingly share
With me, too, when the famine came;
If you had plenty wheat, you'd not give me a tare,
And you wouldn't expose my name.

If you understood me, and I understood you,
I'd always believe what you said;
And there wouldn't be nothing that folks could do
That could put it out of my head;
And you would not doubt, either, the statements I'd make,
Then you'd let others know where you stood;
And whenever some person my bad side would take,
You'd turn in, and show him the good.

–Dedicated to my friend, Prof. W. H. Fuller

A Mood

Today is but tomorrow;
Tomorrow but today;
There is no change in sorrow
To be, or yesterday.

Today is but tomorrow;
Tomorrow but today;
There is no joy to borrow,
Nor pain to turn away.

At the Parting of the Ways

They both were reared in the village,
And grew up in the town;
They came from worthy families;
The best that could he found.

They played and worked together,
From morning until night;
They never liked to be apart,
But in each others sight.

Their friendship but grew stronger
As the months and years passed by;
Their comradeship grew dearer
Beneath a clear blue sky.

But, alas, there came a parting,
They both must leave the town;
So Joe chose the upward path,
And Jim the path leads down.

So Joe he reached the halls of fame
While Jim he brought despair;
'Twas Joe who lived above all blame
And Jim who dealt unfair.

In every case it happens
At the parting of the ways;
One takes the road to failure,
And one the road that pays.

Southern Sunset

The landscape frills, on southern hills,
Have turned a rosy hue;
From rocks, and rills, the night bird trills
The dying day adieu.

Still further west, with added zest,
King Sol vacates his throne;
And dusk does rest, birds hunt their nest
Each soul mate seeks his own.

Away Down Home

I can hear the cowbells tinkling
In the meadow near the dell;
I can see the stars a twinkling
To the rhythm of the bell;
I can hear the doves a cooing
As they nestle on some bough,
And the whippoorwill a wooing
His fair mate beside the slough;
Away down home.

I can see the sun ascending
Oer the eastern plains so green,
And its rays so gently bending
To add beauty to the scene;
I can hear the gentle zephyrs
As they whisper songs of glee;
Wafting sweet perfume that pleases
From the flowers o'er the lea;
Away down home.

I can hear the old night owl
Perched upon some lonely tree;
Give a hoot and then a scowl
'Cause the daylight's soon to be;
I can see the robin redbreast
Squatting on the old lane fence;
Singing what he calls his best
As on barley he does mince;
Away down home.

I can see the moon a' shining,
Kissing all the stars goodnight;
All her rays of love confining
On the earth to make it bright;

Lighting up to cheer all mortals
From the twilight to the dawn,
Until day shall ope her portals,
And shall usher in the morn;
Away down home.

I Love the Old Songs

I love the old songs, full of grace,
That brought God to an enslaved race,
And loosened from King Bondage's ties
Downtrodden souls with plaintive cries.

I love the old songs' jubilees,
That used to float o'er brooks, through trees,
To God who, seated on His throne,
Sent back the word: "You're not
alone."

I love the old songs, soul-felt lays
That rendered unto God his praise;
So full of pathos, maybe queer,
But yet they brought the Savior near.

I love tbe old songs, songs of yore,
That soothed the heart when backs were sore,
And sent God from his throne above
To free a people with his love.

My Song

There are others who sing of the beauty
Of the things constructed by man;
But, I sing just for love, not for honor
Of the works of the Father's hand.

There are some who may sing of the
grandeur
And beauty of hand-painted scrolls;
But I sing of the cliff and the brooklet;
The clear, sparkling water, and shouls.

There appear those who sing of the graces,
Of cities with pleasures and gains;
But I sing of the oak, and the willow,
And the beauty of plateaus and plains.

Oh, the others may sing of the comforts of life,
And the luxuries which now exist;
But my song shall be of the winds and the waves,
The sunlight, the dew, and the mist.

The songs of the others may glimmer, and shine
With the sweetness of music and art;
But to sing of the moonlight night, and
the stars
And their glory shall be my part.

A Passing Fancy

I am glad for the beauty that lives.
For the sun-kissed tops of the mountain range;
For the canyon so droll, and its beauty;
For the seasons we have, and their change;
For the man who fulfills every duty.

For the sparrow who sings to lighten;
For the water lilies in the lake;
For the moon, and stars that brighten;
For the sunflowers when they awake.

For the forests so mystic, and haunting;
For the rivulets meandering by;
For the whippoorwill's music he's vaunting;
For the raindrops that fall from on high.

For the doves and all of their cooing;
For the willows that bend o'er the creek;
For the souls that are intent on wooing;
For the snowfield that covers the peak.

I am glad for the beauty that lives.

Midday Reflections

If 'twere mine to forget the sorrow
That the past has apportioned me;
If I but knew what the morrow
And her donation would be;
I know that the consolation
These longings must always bring;
Would mean the eradication
Of many a bitter sting.

If 'twere mine to retain the gladness
Of the days that have long since flown;
If 'twere mine to know the sadness
That is soon to be my own;
I am sure that the revealing
Of the incidents to be
Would but hasten my ill-feeling
Towards fate and destiny.

The Flower Rare

I went into my garden
In search of nature's best
I thought before selecting
Just which will meet the test.

I looked about in wonder,
And saw the lovely rose;
The flower that everybody
Thinks is the best that grows.

I gazed in bold amazement
At violets so proud;
They, too, won admiration;
With sweetest scent endowed.

My eyes behold the pansy;
So sweet and pure it seemed;
In all her gayest colors,
This caused my eyes to beam.

Carnations grew beside me;
They made a pretty sight;
I felt my heart beat faster,
And laughed with sheer delight.

Then, turning in my pathway,
I saw the lily fair;
My heart enraptured told me
This is the flower rare.

Heart's Solitude

Ere man has crossed the threshold of the great and fair beyond;
There must come times when in his heart he feels sad and forlorn;
Some days will dawn with sorrow, sadness, anguish and despair;
This hour that comes, and lingers long, cries to thy Heart beware.

Ere man has done his mission, that the savior bade him do;
There comes a day into his life, when not a friend is true;
The heart in exile yearns intensely for some kindred spirit just,
But now, alas, no answer comes, from out the dust to dust.

Ere man has finished here the race of life which he's begun;
In solitude his heart must dwell, before some setting sun;
No sympathetic hearts will vibrate through the air all will be dark.
So on its long and weary journey, it must alone embark.

A Night Supreme

A silent night when stillness holds full sway,
And constellations shine in brighter hue;
When atmosphere holds clouds and mists at bay,
And breezes mild have put to flight the dew.
A night where myriads of shining stars
Promulgate with their radiance so fair;
A scene of beauty that no milk-maid mars,
And sweet perfume of flowers fills the air.
A night when all the sky is bright;
The full moon sending forth exhorbant rays,
And showing plainly as it sheds its light
An earthly paradise enthroned in agate haze.

A Donation

She gave me a smile today,
A balm to soothe the heart;
Upon my soul it played;
I begged it not depart.
She gave me a hand-clasp too,
Which thrilled me o'er and o'er
With sweet responses true;
I bade it come once more.
She gave me a cunning glance
From out her deep brown eyes;
As gaily they did dance
I dreamed of azure skies.
She gave me a rose today
With perfumed petals white;
Its fragrance so enchanted me;
I waked not through the night.

--THREE--
THE NEGRO IN TEXAS HISTORY

This fifteen page booklet was not only filled with the script that follows but with numerous photographs and a few drawings, but they would not reprint well and so are not included. The cover design refers to "one hundred years of Negro progress in Texas." Brewer was knowledgeable about and proud of black Texas accomplishments over the previous century. Though we have not included the photos, we have included Brewer's descriptions of the individuals and the buildings that were included in his fascinating study. One photo was of the Texas Negro Hall of Fame that numerous black Texans sought and were pleased with its inclusion in the Texas centennial. It should be noted that a similar document was provided for the Texas sesquicentennial; it was edited by Jesse E. Gloster and Hunter O. Brooks and titled *The Black Presence in the Texas Sesquicentennial* (Houston: D. Armstrong Company, 1986).

Originally published as J. Mason Brewer, *An Historical and Pictorial Souvenir of The Negro in Texas History in Celebration of the Texas Centennial 1836–1936*. Dallas: Mathis Publishing, 1935. Reprinted with permission.

***

Author's Introductory Statement

From the period of Exploration in 1528 until 1935, an expanse of four hundred and eighty years, the history of the part the Negro has played in the development of Texas has been glorious as well as glamorous. It would be impossible to tell the true story of Texas without including the various contributions made by the black race at frequent intervals to the building of this great empire. Hail Texas! Hail the Texas Negro!

—J. Mason Brewer

Episode 1
The Negro in Texas Exploration
1528 – 1539

In the year 1527, the Spanish King commissioned one Panfilo de Narvaez to command a fleet which was sent to explore the North American country north of Tampico and east to Florida. The fleet was lost in the Gulf of Mexico, and some of the crew with Alvar Nunez Cabeza de Vaca, who accompanied the expedition as official treasurer, were cast on the coast.

Among those whose lives were saved was a Negro Arab Moor by the name of Estavanico who came to be known as little Stephen. Estavanico was one of the three men who first explored Texas. His two companions were Cabeza de Vaca and another Spaniard by the name of Pablo Dorantes. These three men wandered over the territory now known as Texas from the Sabine river to the Rio Grande. During this time they were captured and enslaved by the Indians and lived on prickly pear, roots and pecans. They finally escaped and reached the interior of Mexico.

Later in 1539 Estavanico was employed by the Mexican Viceroy, Don Antonio Mendoza, to head a return expedition over the Cabeza de Vaca trail. He was accompanied by a Franciscan Friar, Father Marco. Stephen remained far in advance of the expedition. He sent back word daily to the Friar to hurry on, informing him about the wonders of the country he was traversing. When he was thirty days journey ahead he sent a message to the Friar urging him to hurry on, saying that he had found a mighty province called Ceuela or Cibola. He was slain. Little Stephen was one of the first martyrs for the cause of Texas Exploration and is credited by some with the discovery of New Mexico.

Episode 2
The Era of Slave Traffic
1816 – 1820

Negro slaves were sold into Texas before the state had been colonized, and slave labor introduced. The first Negroes were brought to Texas by Louis de Aury, who established a slave market on Galveston Island in 1816. With seven ships he combed the waters of the West Indies in order to rob the slave ships coming to the Americas. By this method of Piracy great numbers of slaves were brought to Galveston Island and sold to slave dealers and planters in Louisiana. The majority of them were sold in New Orleans, for at this time Texas was not settled and an outside market had to be found for the disposal of the slaves.

Jean Lafitte, the pirate, built the town of Campeche on the present site of Galveston in the same year de Aury started the slave traffic enterprise and continued the theft and sale of slaves begun by him. In the year 1818 Lafitte was joined by the Bowie brothers. From 1818 to 1820 the Bowie brothers alone are said to have made a net profit of $65,000 off of the sale of slaves.

Episode 3
The Pre-colonization Period
1820 – 1821

In the year 1819 James Long, a young physician of Natchitoches, Louisiana, inspired by the De Onis Treaty by which Texas was traded for Florida, decided to occupy Texas and claim it as a part of Louisiana. He organized an expedition and established a settlement at Bolivars Point at the end of the peninsula, across the channel from Galveston Island. In 1820 he returned to Bolivar, accompanied by his young wife. Mrs. Long brought with her a 12-year-old Negro girl by the name of Kian. After a few months General Long went to Mexico, taking with him most of his men. Mrs. Long, with her little daughter Ann, and the Negro slave girl were left with twenty-five men to await his return. When General Long did not return at the end of a few months, the men began to leave singly and in groups until at the end of a year Mrs. Long, her daughter, and Kian the Negro girl were left alone. For weeks the only food they had consisted of birds that Mrs. Long shot. During the winter the bay was frozen and Kian caught fish in the ice for their food.

After Mrs. Long received the news of the death of her husband in Mexico she became a member of one of Stephen F. Austin's first colonies. Kian, the Negro slave girl, remained with her and one of Kian's sons became an Overseer for Mrs. Jane H. Long. Mrs. Long is called the Mother of Texas. Kian Long might well be called the Mother of Negro Texans, having served as a slave in Texas before Stephen F. Austin established the first colony.

Episode 4
The Era of Slave Labor
1821 – 1865

The first cargo of slaves was actually sold into Texas in the year 1821. Prior to this time Texas was a wilderness and there was no particular need for slaves. Stephen F. Austin at this time obtained a grant from the Mexican Government to settle a colony of three hundred families. This settlement was established at the present site of Old Washington on the Brazos in Washington County. The first slaves in Texas toiled here.

Negro Slave Labor in the early development of Texas consisted of the clearing of forests, and the cultivation of cotton and rice. These early settlements were located in the Trinity, Sabine, Neches, and Colorado river bottoms. Some of the most fertile soil in America was to be found in these sections. Slave labor, therefore, was very profitable.

Descendants of Kian
Clarissa Smith, daughter of Kian Long
Kian Jackson, daughter of Clarissa Smith and

granddaughter of Kian Long. She furnished data for Sowell's *History of Fort Bend County*.

Jim Long, son of Kian Long. He was Overseer during slavery for Mrs. Jane Long, his mother's mistress, with whom she came to Texas in 1820. He lived in Richmond, Texas, for many years after Emancipation. Others in group are his wife, daughter and son. He died in San Antonio in the early 1890s.

Rebecca Breed, granddaughter of Kian, her son Henry C. Breed who is a veteran Police Officer in Houston, Texas, his wife and little daughter.

Episode 5
The Negro in the Texas Revolution
1836

One of the most heroic struggles for Texas independence from Mexico took place on March 6, 1836, when a small group of Texans under the command of William Barrett Travis attempted to defend the historic Alamo in San Antonio against the attack of Santa Anna, the Mexican General. The Mexicans had 4,000 men taking part in the fight which ensued, while the Texans only numbered one hundred eighty men. The courage, valor, and loyalty displayed by these men who died for Texas Liberty is one of the most outstanding examples of heroism in world history.

Texas was trying at this time to gain her independence from Mexico and Col. Travis and his men had been trapped in the Alamo without a chance to receive re-enforcements to aid them in fighting the enemy. All of the people in the fort were killed with the exception of the wife of Lieutenant Dickenson, one of the officers, a few Mexican women with their children, and a Negro slave who was the only male survivor of the Alamo. In the Capitol at Austin is a painting of the Alamo and the Negro survivor holding the Texas flag on high.

Episode 6
Negro Emancipation in Texas
1865

Although the Emancipation Proclamation freeing thousands of Negro slaves in the United States was issued January 1, 1863, many months passed before the slaves in the Southern states were actually given their freedom. The dates of actual emancipation vary in all of these states.

On May 29, 1865, General Sheridan was assigned to the command of the Military Division of the Southwest, headquarters at New Orleans. On June 10, he ordered General Gordon Granger to proceed with the 1,800 men to Galveston. General Granger arrived at Galveston on June 19, 1865, and immediately in conformity to instructions assumed command of all forces in the state and issued orders declaring that by proclamation of the President all slaves were free.

Since June 19, 1865, the Negroes in Texas have celebrated the date of their freedom with great enthusiasm. Programs, usually held in the open, are conducted, and great rejoicing is manifested on this day. The ex-slaves are always given special places on the program and special seats on the platforms. Songs, band music, the reading of the Emancipation Proclamation, and speaking, share equally in the days celebration. Always there is a barbeque and watermelons add to the pleasure of the occasion. The Negroes in Texas call this day's observance "Juneteenth".

Episode 7
The Negro in Texas Reconstruction,
Legislatures, and Politics
1868 – 1896

The enfranchisement of the Negro freedmen in Southern states in the year 1865 gave them the right to vote and hold office. Since Southern Confederates and their sympathizers were disenfranchised by the Federal Constitution for a short period at this time the white

Republicans and Negro freedmen formed the majority group. This fact caused the Negro to have extensive political power and led to his election as representative and Senator in the various Southern states.

In Texas during the period from 1868 to 1895 forty-six Negroes served as Legislators. Three Negroes, G. T. Ruby, Matt Gaines, and W. M. Burton, served as Senators. Thirteen were members of Constitutional Conventions and many were representatives from different districts. During this time they helped pass legislation which proved helpful to the state as well as their race. They were above the average in intelligence of their race for the period in which they served. These Negroes served on committees, voted wisely, and were authors of many bills which passed and became laws. On one occasion during the convening of the Twenty-fourth Legislature in 1895 two Negro Representatives, R. L. Smith and N. H. Haller, kept the State of Texas from becoming bankrupt by changing their nay votes to yea. Norris Wright Cuney, another Texas Negro, was for many years the political boss of the Republican party in Texas.

Norris Wright Cuney was the most outstanding political leader of his race in Texas. He was born in Waller County, Texas, in 1846. He entered politics in 1869. In the year 1872 he was elected delegate to the Republican National Convention. In 1875 he was appointed secretary of Republican State Executive Committee. The height of his political career came from 1876 to 1880. He served as Collector of Customs for the port of Galveston and is responsible for the establishment of a Deaf, Dumb and Blind Institute for Negroes in the State of Texas.

There were six Negro members of the Constitutional Convention of 1875 which framed the present Texas Constitution. Four of them are found on the present photograph. Third row, left to right—No. 8, David Abner. Fourth row, left to right—No. 9, William Reynolds. No. 10, B. B. Davis. Fifth row, left to right—No. 2, John Mitchell.

Episode 8
The Era of Negro Progress

The Negro population in Texas at the present time (c. 1935) is 854,964. 329,879 of this number live in cities. 409,879 constitute the rural farm population and 115,213 comprise the rural non-farm group.

Negros in the state own 85,612 farms. Farming is their chief occupation. In some counties Negroes own approximately three or four times as many farms as whites. An example of this is Harrison County, where Negroes have outnumbered whites since the existence of slavery. There are 6,802 farms in this county. Negroes own 4,990 of them while whites own only 1,812. Through the agency of county extension agents Negro farmers in Texas have been trained to get the best results from their planting. They have also been taught how to improve their production and control their marketing.

Education in Texas for Negroes is engaging more and more attention for those responsible for the administration of its needs. The present scholastic group numbers 259,025. 5,227 Negro public school teachers are employed. There are 224 Principals of Public Schools. Of this number 141 are High School principals, two are Junior High School principals and 81 are Elementary School Principals. Negroes have six Private or Denominational Colleges, one Municipal Junior College at Houston, Texas, and an Episcopal Junior College, St. Phillip's Junior College in San Antonio. They have six Senior Colleges. Approximately 1,600 students attend these colleges annually.

Houston has the largest Negro population in the state. Approximately 70,000 Negros live in the city. San Antonio has a modern City Auditorium for Negroes. Houston has more than 100 Negro Mail Carriers. Galveston has twelve Negro Policemen. Dallas has a $185,000 Y.M.C.A. Building. Austin has a beautiful Park and Recreational center and Community center. Ft. Worth is noted for its fine Negro

Churches and has a Modern Negro Hotel.

There are more than 500,000 Baptists in Texas and approximately 32,000 Methodists and 42,000 Negroes who are members of the African Methodist Episcopal.

(Following are Brewer's descriptions of persons and places in photos we were unable to reproduce.)

Top Row

The home of the late Grand Chancellor W. S. Willis. The late Grand Chancellor W. S. Willis of the Knights of Pythias was a graduate of Bishop College. When he was elected Grand Chancellor the organization was $75,000 in debt and at the time of his death the organization was in the million dollar class. His widow, Mrs. W. S. Willis, Jr., took a trip around the world in the spring of 1933. Mrs. Willis is actively interested in all movements of uplift.

The home of Mr. Heads, near Carrollton, Texas. Mr. Heads is one of the most progressive farmers in the vicinity of Dallas. Mr. C. A. Walton is the County Agent and is doing constructive work with the farmers in this district.

The home of Mr. and Mrs. Calvin P. Christian. Mr. Christian is an excellent auto mechanic and during the World War served his country as a soldier with the American Expeditionary Forces. Mrs. Christian, who was Miss Ola Smith before her marriage, is a finished seamstress and is an ex-student of the Dallas High School. Mr. Christian has oil interests in Gregg County and is interested in all movements for race betterment. Mr. and Mrs. Christian have one child, a little daughter Rachel.

Second Row

The Greater St. James Baptist Church, Fort Worth, Texas. One of Texas' greatest churches. Dr. J. H. Winn, pastor. Dr. J. H. Winn was called to the pastorate of the Greater St. James Baptist Church in the month of February, 1911. At this time the church was eight hundred dollars in debt with a membership of less than one hundred. During the twenty-four years of his leadership the church membership has risen to more than four thousand with the church owing a black of ground fully equipped with four upright pianos, one baby grand piano, a pipe organ, bath rooms for men and women, with a park suitable for all social and open air meetings.

Third Row

St. Peters Academy, founded in 1908, has served Dallas and vicinity for twenty-seven years. Elementary and High School courses are offered.

The Houston Branch of the National Alliance of Postal Employees. There are 175 Postal Employees of this group working in or out of the Houston Post Office, 92 of whom are members of the Houston Branch of the N.A.P.E. The officers of the Houston Branch are as follows: Frank L. Lane, Pres.; C. W. Hicks, Jr., Vice PRES.; w. d. Powell, Financial Secy.; S. L. Payne, Recording Secy.; A. Youngblood, Treas.; T. B. Allen, Reporter and Rev. Earnest Sheparp, Chaplain.

The Pinkston Clinic, founded by Dr. L. G. Pinkston in 1928. The Pinkston Clinic is serving a real need in Dallas. A competent corps of workers are employed.

Fourth Row

The Moorland Branch Y.M.C.A., Dallas, Texas. The Moorland Branch Y.M.C.A. was erected in the year 1931 at a cost of $185,000. It is one of the largest and best equipped Y.M.C.A. buildings in the United States.

Wheatley Elementary School. The Wheatley Elementary School of Dallas was built in 1929. It is one of the most modern school buildings in the State. William Jackson is the competent Principal.

Prominent Dallas Negroes

Top Row

The Dunbar Branch Library was opened to the public on July 1, 1933. Mrs. A. B. Venters, the present Librarian, was placed in charge at that time and has through her enthusiasm and planning created intense interest in reading among the Negro population of Dallas. The library contains approximately 6,000 volumes, covering a large variety of subjects. The Booker T. Washington High School Ambassadors. Texas' leading High School Choral Club was organized in 1927 by Mr. A. S. Jackson, Director of Music of the Booker T. Washington High School. The Club is composed of 50 picked voices. They have sung before the International Rotary Convention and every important educational organization in the state.

Second Row

H. Strickland, President and founder of the Excelsior Mutual Life Insurance Co. Mr. Strickland has built up the largest institution of its kind in the state. The company at the present time employs two hundred and five race men and women. The company has paid since its organization in 1912 $7,000,000 in sick and death claims. In 1935 Mr. Strickland was voted the most useful Negro citizen in Dallas. A. Maceo Smith, Executive Secretary of the Dallas Negro Chamber of Commerce. Teacher of Commerce at the Booker T. Washington High School. Under his direction the Negro Chamber of Commerce has become the aggressive factor it is in behalf race welfare in Dallas. He appeared before the Texas legislature to request a fair representation of the Negro's contribution in the progress and history of Texas at the "Texas Centennial." A.A. Braswell, Executive Vice President of the Crawford Undertaking Co. Leader of the Negro Division of the Red cross Drive in Dallas for the year 1935. Mr. Braswell is an alert and civic minded business man. He has proven himself an efficient and capable executive by successfully managing one of the biggest and most up to date business firms in the entire southwest. C. E. Smith, Founder and Director of the Educational Forum for Negroes in Dallas. Junior member of the Committee of Management of the Y.M.C.A.. President of the City Federation of B.T.U.'s. Inspiring and helpful information has been consistently made available to the Dallas Negro public through the vision of Mr. Smith. Joseph McMillan, Principal of York Elementary School. Mr. McMillan is a close student of educational trends and and affairs and a competent and energetic school man. Mrs. I. Pauline Ward. Business Woman. Manufacturer. Beautician. Mrs. Ward is owner of the "Unique Beauty Salon" and is the manufacturer of "Lady Pauline Face and Hair Preparations." She is one of the most outstanding and progressive business women in the state. James J. Thompson, Artist, Teacher. Mr. Thompson drew the sketch asorning the cover page of this Souvenir. He is a teacher at Garland, Texas, and lives in Dallas. Rev. R. T. Andrews, Pastor of St. Johns Baptist Church. Treasurer of the National Moderators Association. Head of the NAACP drive in Dallas for the year 1935. He is a grandson of one Texas Negro Legislators. Rev. P. F. Jackson, Pastor St. James A.M.E. Church. Secretary of the Inter-denominational Ministerial Alliance. During the two years he has served as pastor at St. James he has reduced the church debt from $51,000 to $29,000.

Third Row
Mrs. W. E. Shallowhorne. President of the Parent Teachers Association of Booker T. Washington High School. Mrs. Shallowhorne is probably the most active woman in Dallas of her group as regards civic betterment. Miss Marion Hill, Executive secretary of the Maria Morgan Branch Y.W.C.A.. Miss Hill is an energetic and efficient Secretary, A. S. Wells, Grand Attorney for the Knights of

Pythias. Atorney Wells came into National prominence in the spring of 1935 when he ran for office of representative to the Texas legislature from Dallas Cunty. Mr. Wells polled 1,001 votes and won fifth place. Dr. William Green. Physician and Surgeon. Founder of The Green Chair, established in 1930. Owner of Green Building. Member Board of Directors Negro Chamber of Commerce. C. F. Carr, Principal of J. P. Starks Elementary School. Mr. Carr was the first principal of the present Booker T. Washington High School. He has been President of the State Teachers Association. L. Virgil Williams, Principal of the Booker T. Washington High School. Chairman Court of Honor of the Boy Scouts. Chairman Boys Work Committee, Moorland Branch, Y.M.C.A. Member Board of Directors of the dallas negro Chamber of Commerce. Member State Advisory Committee of N.Y.A. Contributor to National Educational Journal and National Race magazines. Mr. Williams is easily the most progressive High School Executive in the state. During his administration the extra-curricular organizations of his school have increased from four to twenty-three and the school enrollment from 452 to 1759. Rev. W. L. Cash, Pastor of the Plymouth Congregational Church. Chairman of Negro Division of the Community Chest Drive for Dallas in 1935. Formerly President of the National Convention of Congregational Work among colored people and Assistant Moderator of the National Council of Congregational Church of the United States. Mrs. H. D. Winn, Civic and Religious leader. Member of Negro Centennial Committee. Director, Negro Chamber of Commerce. Trustee of Bethel A.M.E. Church.

Fourth Row

Rev. L. L. Haynes, Pastor St. Paul Methodist Church. President of Inter-denominational Ministers Alliance of Dallas. Member Board of Directors of the Negro Chamber of Commerce. Member of Committee of United Charities of the City of Dallas. Member of State Inter-racial Committee. Registrar of the Board of Examiners of the West Texas Annual Conference of the Methodist Episcopal Church. Miss P. L. Tyler, Teacher of Spanish in the Booker T. Washington High School. Organizer of the Civic Music Guild. Charter Member and Chairman of the Executive Committee of the G Clef Music Club. President of Ladies Reading Circle. Dr. F. H. Jordan, Physician. Dr. Jordan served his internship at St. Louis City Hospital. He is a Dallasite and has fitted himself to render efficient service in his chosen field. J. B. Richey, Principal of Lincoln Manor School. Mr. Richey is regarded as one of the most roundly educated school principals in the state. William Jackson, Principal of Wheatley Elementary School. Prof. Jackson is a fine type of Optimistic Educator. T. D. Marshall, Principal of B. F. Darrell School. Principal of the Evening School for negroes. Mr. Marshall has more pupils enrolled in his school than any other Negro school in the city. Dr. L. G. Pinkston, Physician and Surgeon. Founder of the Pinkston Clinic. Member, Board of Directors, Negro Chamber of Commerce. The Pinkston Clinic has cared for more than 2,000 bed patients since its organization in 1928.

Fifth Row

Mrs. C. B. Boswell, President, Federated Council of Church Women of the city. Superintendent of Sunday School of Plymouth Congregational Church. Pioneer promoter of Daily Vacation Bible Schools among Dallas churches. Chairman Inter-denominational School of Missions. Member, Committee of Management of the Y.W.C.A. T. W. Pratt, Principal of Julia C. Frazier Elementary School. Ex-President of the State Teachers Association. Dr. R. T. Hamilton, Grand Medical examiner for the Knights of Pythias of Texas. Chairman of the Y.M.C.A. drive for 1935. Dr. Hamilton is the most energetic and forceful worker for race benefits in the city. Robert A. Lee, Grand Master of the St. Anthony A.F. and A.M. Grand Lodge. Commander-in-Chief of the American Colored Veterans Association. Proprietor of the State Street Drug Store. Mr. Lee is the son of the late Rev. R. Lee and inherited considerable oil interests in Rusk County. A. S. Jackson, Jr., Director of Music, Booker T. Washington High School. Chorister New Hope Baptist Church. Teacher of Music. Mrs. A. B. Venters. Teacher. Librarian of Dunbar Branch Library. Mrs. Venters is the first Librarian of the Dunbar Library. Sheis one of the most efficient Librarians in the Southwest.

Bottom Row

The Dallas skyline, looking from Oak Cliff. The Crawford Undertaking Company was founded by the late E. J. Crawford in 1909. It is one of the largest and best equipped funeral homes in the Southwest, serving Dallas over a quarter of a century. Mrs. E. B. Crawford, widow of the late E. J. Crawford, is President-Treasurer of the firm and A. A. Braswell is Executive Vicve President and Manager.

Negro Achievement in Texas

Dr. and Mrs. J. W. Anderson

Dr. J. W. Anderson, Texas' and the nation's leading Negro Philanthropist, has lived in Dallas for forty-seven years. He was born in Lexington, Mo., and attended school at Kansas University. When he reached his Junior year he went the Meharry Medical College and there pursued his studies in medicine which he completed in 1885. In the year 1886, he took a post-graduate course at the University of Michigan. In 1900 he was a Fellow at the American Institute of Phrenology, from which he graduated with honors. While a Senior at Meharry he was an Instructor of Anatomy and after graduation he lectured in the School of Dentistry on the subject of Operative Dentistry. He practiced medicine for three years in Nashville, Tenn., before coming to Dallas, where he has resided since that time.

Mrs. J. W. Anderson is a native of Louisiana and along with her distinguished and philanthropic husband deserves commendation for the active interest she has manifested in the welfare of her race and humanity.

Dr. Anderson has given thousands of dollars to worthy institutions, the most notable being to his Alma Mater, Meharry Medical Collage, Nashville, Tenn., the Moorland Branch Y.M.C.A. at Dallas, Texas, Wiley College at Marshall, Texas, and St. Peters Academy in Dallas. He is intensely interested in the proper development of the youth of his race. He purchased all of the books needed for the introduction of a course in Negro History at the Booker T. Washington High School of Dallas and more recently paid 223 Y.M.C.A. memberships for seventh grade boys of the Elementary schools of Dallas. "Deeds, not Words" is his motto and he himself is a living example of this philosophy. His life and his work are a credit to Texas, his race and the nation.

The Carnegie Library

The Carnegie Library at Wiley College, Marshall, Texas. Wiley College, the leading college for Negroes in Texas and the Southwest, is the State's oldest college, having been established in 1873. It was the first college in the Southwest to receive "A" rating by the Southern Association of Colleges and Secondary Schools. It is the only Negro College west of the Mississippi that has an endowment. Dr. M. W. Dogan, the president of the college, has served the institution forty years. It is largely through his wise leadership and knowledge of educational affairs that Wiley has achieved is present rating as one of the leading colleges for Negroes in the United States.

Father Max Murphy

Father Murphy is the first colored native of Texas to be ordained a Priest. He was born in Dallas and formerly attended St. Peters Academy in Dallas, Texas. He began his studies for the priesthood at Bay, St. Louis, Mo. In 1929 he went to Europe to complete his Theological studies at the German Theological Faculty at the Charles University, Prague, where he graduated June 24, 1934. He was ordained to the Holy Priesthood in the historic and ancient Cathedral of St. Vitus there. He is the first American citizen to receive this honor.

–FOUR–
HERALDING DAWN: AN ANTHOLOGY OF VERSE BY TEXAS NEGROES

Likely the most important contribution made by our book on the Texas writings of J. Mason Brewer is the republication of *Heralding Dawn*. These poems from the black Texas community of the 1920s and 1930s would not be available to readers, researchers, and students were it not for the ability and foresight of J. Mason Brewer. He collected authors of merit, including Lawrence Carlyle Tatum, Bernice Love Wiggins, Clarence F. Carr, and Gwendolyn Bennett. At the beginning of his book Brewer also comments on the historic significance of these and other regional writers.

Originally published as J. Mason Brewer, edited. *Heralding Dawn: An Anthology of Verse by Texas Negroes*. Dallas: June Thomason Printing, 1936. Reprinted by permission.

*****

Donated

To the Booker T. Washington High School,
Dallas, Texas. Date Sept. 15, 1939
Being firm believers in God and Man
And in doing all that we possibly can
To help the young folks of our race
Try to be something and get some place –
We take great pleasure in sending you
Facts inspiring, good, and true
Of Negro Texans who played their part
In building up Texas from the start.
This little book, from first to last
Will acquaint young folks with their peoples' past
And tell them also in a way

About Texas Negroes of Today.
Our hope is that this volume may
Help your students in some way
And inspire some of them to want to be
Great like those in this History.
Sincerely yours,
Mr. and Mrs. D. S. Smith
Dallas, Texas

BIBLIOGRAPHY AND ACKNOWLEDGMENT
Brewer. J. Mason: *Negrito*, San Antonio, 1933.

Tatum, Lawrence Carlyle: *Log Cabin Lyrics*. Los Angles, 1917.

Wiggins, Bernice Love: *Tuneful Tales*. El Paso, 1925.

Acknowledgment for permission to reprint is gratefully made to the following periodicals:

Opportunity (New York), for Gwendolyn Bennett's "On A Birthday".

The Crisis (New York), for Malcolm Christian Conley's "American Ideals".

The Messenger (Chicago), for Malcolm Christian Conley's "Four Walls".

The Dallas Express (Dallas), for R. T. Hamilton's "Sister Mandy Attends the Business League".

The Dallas Express (Dallas), for Maurine Jeffrey's "My Rainy Day".

DEDICATION
To The Mothers and Fathers of All of Us Who
Have Contributed To This Volume

Contents

Gwendolyn Bennett	99
On a Birthday	100
J. Mason Brewer	101
Dew	102
Deep Ellum and Central Track	103
Secon' Pickin'	105
Apostolic	106
Clarence F. Carr	107
The Encampment Choir	108
Malcolm Christian Conley	111
For Mother in Paradise	112
Four Walls	112
American Ideals	113
Lauretta Holman Gooden	114
A Dream of Revenge	115
Question to a Mob	116
Richard T. Hamilton	117
Sister Mandy Attends the Business League	118
A Negro's Prayer	120
Maurine L. Jeffrey	122
My Rainy Day	123
Pappy's Last Song	124
Lillian Tucker Lewis	126
Longing	127
J. Austin Love	128
Out in the Still Wet Night	129
Down Fish Trap Lane	130

Joseph McMillan	131
Death Scene	132
Birdelle Wycoff Ransom	133
Night	134
J. C. Stevenson	135
A Day's Recreation	136
G. T. Smith	137
Watermelon	138
Lawrence Carlyle Tatum	139
Choicy	140
Bernice Love Wiggins	141
Church Folks	142

Preface

For anyone concerned with the impact of one race upon another, these verses have an unusual interest. It is true, as the Editor points out, that they are of uneven quality: and those that are bad are bad in an unpleasant way-by being imitative of the vices of bad verse by white poets. The didactic manner, retailing commonplaces of prudence: the unmastered expression of more or less raw emotion; false 'sublimity'; an occasional echo of the Imagist manner – all these faults can he found in the present collection. But here and there an authentic cry breaks through with the ring of life in it. And there is a sense in which life is always equal to itself, so that there can be no degrees of it or of its true expression. 'Since I Bought My Ticket, Lawdy, Can't I Ride?', these poets seem to be saying, when they can forget the effort to be literary: and the question comes from somewhere deep. The discerning reader will be able to find here the pallet on the floor of a tenant farmer's cabin in the cotton fields: the Jig Saw, born along the Central tracks in Dallas: the Georgia Sweet with meat as red as a pork chop; the Chariot that appeared to the grey old slave on the bank of Israel's Jordan: and once in a while – unexpectedly – the wind of Time blowing softly from nowhere.

For later editions of the anthology, no doubt, a more rigorous principle of selection will be used: but the Editor believes his first task is to give the poets an opportunity to be heard. A native of Texas and a graduate of Wiley College, he has served on the faculty of Samuel Huston College in Austin, and is now a teacher of Spanish at the Booker T. Washington High School in Dallas. In his book of dialect verse, *Negrito*, in a recently published study of the Texas Negro in Reconstruction, and in contributions to the *Publications* of the Texas Folk-Lore Society, he has consistently striven to record the life of Negroes in Texas. Now he is trying to lead others to do the same thing. His venture, it seems to me, deserves to succeed.

–Henry Smith

I. Editor's Note

Recently in various regions of America a tendency to develop schools of regional writers using materials peculiar to their special localities has been responsible for the production of numerous works of great value. Texas is one of the states in which many authors have developed regional tendencies. This has been made more fully manifest through their poetry than through any other medium of literary expression.

White Texas poets have used regional themes to a great extent. The Negroes in Texas who have written verse have also been influenced to some degree by the traditions, life, and customs of their native state and localities. Their poetic efforts have not been limited to this type, however, for many of their productions transcend region and race. This collection of verse written by Texas Negroes does not purport to embrace quantity or necessarily to possess quality. The only claim advanced in presenting this compilation to the public is that it represents the results of conscientious effort and originality on the part of the contributors in their efforts to record their moods, thoughts, impressions and ideals in verse.

No rigid standards were set up by which the individual contributions were judged fit or unfit for inclusion in this volume. An attempt was made, however, to include the best efforts and select as large a variety of forms and subjects as possible. Many of the selections appearing here were first published in national magazines and newspapers. Some of them, no doubt, have real merit.

As rich as Texas is in material for those interested in writing about Negro life, very little has been written about the Negro in Texas. This is due partly to the fact that the Negro in Texas as a subject for literature has been obscured by other subjects equally as colorful and interesting. The cowboy, the Indian, the Mexican, the pirate, and lost mines and buried treasures, have engaged the attention of white writers to such an extent that the Negro has been almost entirely neglected as subject matter. The Texas Negro himself has been unmindful of the vast possibilities which lie at his hand for writing about his own life. He has failed to realize the rare opportunity he has here to play the role of pioneer.

It is to be hoped that this volume will inspire Texas Negroes of today to accomplish greater things in the field of poetry.

–J. *Mason Brewer*

II. Verse-Making By Negroes in Texas, Historical Summary

The poetic impulse of Texas Negroes found expression first through the medium of Negro dialect, under the influence of Paul Lawrence Dunbar, and most of the early productions were humorous.

Chief among pioneers in this field was C. F. Carr, a native Texan, and a graduate of Wilberforce University at Wilberforce, Ohio. While he was a student at this institution he met Paul Lawrence Dunbar and as a result of this meeting spent much time in Dunbar's company at Dayton, where the poet made his home. Carr was the first Negro in the state to give itinerant recitals of his own compositions. His favorite selection was "When Dad Cooks Soda Biscuits".

G. T. Smith, a native of Indiana, who had lived for a few years in Dayton, was also well acquainted with Dunbar. Mr. Smith came to Texas in 1891 and was one of the first Negroes in the state who wrote acceptable verse. His "Watermelon" delighted many audiences, both during this period and in later years.

Another native Texan among early Negro writers in Texas was Eddie T. Yerwood, a brilliant young school teacher who died in the height of his teaching career. Yerwood was likewise an ardent admirer of Dunbar's work. He entertained many groups with his "A Naught's a Naught and a Figger's a Figger. All fer de White Man an' Nuthin' Fer De Nigger," and other selections in dialect.

The work of the next period of Negro verse-making in Texas was predominantly religious in tone. J. Austin Love, Mrs. Josie Hall and D. L. Williams, a blind evangelist, were the most prominent writers of this period.

After the vogue of religious verse-making came a period of eulogistic verse. States, the race, the nation, and individuals, were eulogized by most of those who wrote verse at this time.

Meanwhile the minds of the Negroes who were interested in developing their poetic talent had already begun to turn to the classics. The study of Latin in the schools had a great fascination for them and caused them to attempt verses using Latin rides. "Multum in Parvo"' and other similar titles were very much in evidence.

Immediately following this epoch the Texas Negro began delving into the philosophy of life and much philosophical verse was produced. Dr. J. W. Fridia of Waco, Texas, was prominent among these versifiers. One of his best known poems was "The Will To Do", the first verse of which is quoted herewith.

The Negroes in Texas who are writing verse at the present time are still using all of the type of verse that have been mentioned heretofore as mediums of expression, but they are also experimenting with new forms, free and metrical, and with new subjects. They speak in terms of the universal, but they also take more cognizance of life in the local communities. Much verse is being written in literary English as well as in Negro dialect.

If the Negro in Texas is to make a distinct contribution in verse to local literature, it must be through the use of materials drawn from the crude life of the Texas Negro – the life of the masses, of the working class in the cities and in the rural districts. He will have to portray the life that he knows best and that others are least acquainted with. This life must be pictured exactly as it is, without any camouflaging. This will necessarily involve the superstitions, customs and traditions of the Texas Negro. This does not mean, however, that the medium of expression must be Negro dialect; most of the verse may well be written in literary English, though some of it can and will be done best through the medium of Negro dialect.

At present there are several outlets for Texas Negroes who feel that they are gifted in verse making. *The Informer*, a Negro weekly published in Houston, through its Junior Informer page and its "Dream Ship", offers an excellent opportunity for Negroes, young and old, to try their hand at recording their thoughts in rhyme. Another organization, an extra-curricular club of the Booker T. Washington High School at Dallas, known as the Bellerophon Quill Club, has published two books of verse written by its members, and has stimulated work along this line among the entire student personnel. In the summer of 1934 a class in Creative Writing was conducted by Professor T. C. Meyers at the Samuel Huston-Tillotson College Summer School, from which a few commendable poems resulted.

More and more the Texas Negro is becoming conscious of his gift of expressing himself in verse, though at the same time he has realized his limitations. This is an indication that he is interested in improving his technique and is likely to arrive.

–J. Mason Brewer

Gwendolyn Bennett

Gwendolyn Bennett was born in Giddings, Texas, July 8, 1902. Her father was a lawyer and her mother a school teacher. She received her elementary education in the public schools of Washington. D. C. She finished a girls' high school in Brooklyn, New York, in 1921. She has studied in the Fine Arts Department of Columbia University, and at one time was an instructor in the Fine Arts Department at Howard University. She has served on the editorial staff of *Opportunity Magazine* in New York City. Miss Bennett became nationally known as an artist and a poetess. Having been born in Texas, Texans feel that they have a claim on her and that the beautiful and poignant lyrics she writes have resulted partially from the impressions of her early Texas surroundings.

On A Birthday

Angels craving for a lark
Rubbed the stars to make a spark.
Pelted Jake and sea with pearls
Just to see them break in swirls.
Combed the hair of hilltop trees
Just to hear their singing breeze.
Whispered low to birds on wing
Just to hear them trill and sing:
Laughed to see the Summer go,
Reveled in the song of snow,
Played with bird and flower and hill –

To find their souls were thirsting still,
And then they took the spark of star,
The swirl of sea, the pearls from far,
The song of trees and birds in flight,
The shout of sun, the calm of night,
The urge that makes the winter pass,
The poetry of sighing grass,
The hush of snow, the laugh of rain,
The ache of joy, the pool of pain:
The sunshine and the shadow, too –
They mixed them well and fashioned you!

(Reprinted from *Opportunity*.)

Dew

The Lord looked down
From His heaven on yesterday:
He saw the sad plight His children on earth were in.
And He cried so much late last night that his tears
Fell down on the grass –
Soon this morning.

                (Not previously published.)

Deep Ellum and Central Track

Talk erbout Harlem ef yuh wants tuh.
An' Lennox Avenue –
But Ah got sumpin' now, Baby.
An kin talk about too.
Harlem's got hits browns an' hits yallers
And sealskin mamas in black,
But 'tain't got nothin' on Dallas,
Deep Ellum an' Central Track.
Harlem's got hits gin and hits whiskey –
Uh li'l penthouse o' two:
But Ah'm still tellin' you. Baby,
Dallas got sumpin', too.
Now hit mought not be no apartment –
Mought be uh "shot-gun" shack:
But de gals sho makes you 'member
Deep Ellum an' Central Track.
Done been all eroun' yo' big State Street,
Uh way up dere in Chi:
An' hits uh putty good hang-out –
Baby, dat ain't no lie.
Gals up dere do de snakehips,
On de streets fuh uh fac':
But gimme mah gal an' de Jig Saw –
Deep Ellum an' Central Track.
      (Not previously published.)

J. MASON BREWER

The editor of *Heralding Dawn*, J. Mason Brewer, has an unusual cultural background for one of his race who is a native Texan. He was born in Goliad, Texas, where his father was a grocer and his mother a teacher in the public schools. Of the six children all are college trained and four are teachers, one sister, Mrs. S. L. Brookes, with an A. M. degree from the University of Michigan, being an instructor in English at Clark University, Atlanta, Georgia.

Mr. Brewer himself, after graduation from high school in Austin, Texas, took his bachelor's degree at Wiley College in 1917, where he was elected class poet. The war took him away from a teacher's desk in the Austin High School and sent him abroad with the American forces, where he acted as company clerk and interpreter. Back in the United States, he returned to teaching in the Ft. Worth schools, becoming a principal in his last year there. A year's work as a clerk in the executive offices of the Continental Oil Company in Denver, Colorado, interrupted only briefly his teaching career, for he returned to Austin, serving first in the high school and then as professor of romance languages in the Samuel Huston College. He is now instructor of Spanish in Booker T. Washington High School of Dallas. He has done graduate work at Denver University and at the University of Colorado.

In spite of Mr. Brewer's busy career as a teacher, he has always shown a driving zeal for creative scholarship and literary work, he has contributed short stories and poems to many periodicals, he has written a pageant on the education of the Negro, he has read papers before the Texas Folklore Society and the National Association for the Study of Negro Life and History, he has published a volume of his own poems in Negro dialect, *Negrito*, he has published a historical volume entitled *"Negro Legislators of Texas and Their Descendants"*, and with *Heralding Dawn* he has gained the enviable distinction of editing the first anthology of Negro verse published in Texas. Combining in rare measure the talent of the scholar with that of the creative author, Mr. Brewer might quite pardonably lay claim to the title of leading man of letters of his race in Texas.

—John Lee Brooks
Southern Methodist University, July 11, 1935

Secon' Pickin'

Secon' pickin's ovuh,
    Secon' pickin's thoo;
Secon' pickin's ovuh –
    Bring de pallet, Sue.

Secon' pickin's ovuh,
    Cotton aint no mo':
Bring de pallet tuh me:
    Put it on de flo'.

Secon' pickin's ovuh,
    Top crop got fros'-bit:
Has yuh got de pallet?
    What un did yuh git?

Secon' pickin's ovuh,
    Secon' pickin's thoo;
Secon' pickin's ovuh –
    Take off bof mah shoe.

Secon' pickin's ovuh,
    Ain't uh boll dat's white:
Ah kin 'joy dis pallet
    Rail shonuff ternite.

        (Not previously published.)

Apostolic

Swaying of bodies, clapping of hands,
Moaning of voices, unknown-tongue commands:
Weird and uncanny gesticulations of a piano-player
As he moves his fingers frantically over the piano keys,
And a seething mass of black, brown and yellow beings
Shouting tunes, mysterious mixtures of Jazz, Religious,
    and Jungle melodies.

Swaying of bodies, clapping of hands,
Moaning of voices, unknown-tongue commands:
Since I bought my ticket, Lawdy, can't I ride?
Oh, since I bought my ticket, Lawdy, can't I ride,
Ride up in de chariot in de mawnin', Lawd?
Swaying of bodies, clapping of hands,
Moaning of voices, unknown-tongue commands:
Things I use tuh do, I don't do no mo' –
Things I use tuh do, I don't do no mo'.
Oh, since I bought my ticket, Lawdy, can't I ride?
Oh, since I bought my ticket, Lawdy, can't I ride,
Ride up in de chariot in de mawnin', Lawd?
Swaying of bodies, clapping of hands,
Moaning of voices, unknown tongue commands.
    (Not previously published.)

Clarence F. Carr

Clarence F. Carr was born in Crockett, Texas, February 26, 1880. He completed his elementary education in the public schools of this city. Afterwards he went to Wilberforce University, Wilberforce, Ohio, where he completed his college education. In the year 1918 he was awarded the honorary degree of Master of Arts by this institution at the same time Mary McLeod Bethune was given this honor, and other notables, including Col. Charles Young and Hon. Emmett J. Scott, were awarded the degree L.L.D. For twelve years he was principal of the Palestine, Texas, high school, and for the past sixteen years he has been principal of various schools in Dallas, including the Booker T. Washington High School. He was the first principal to preside over this school on its present site. He was at one time president of the State Teachers Association. He was chief among the Negro pioneer verse-makers of Texas and often contributed to white dailies. An excerpt from the *Palestine Daily Herald* in 1918 follows:

Prof. Clarence F. Carr, colored principal of Lincoln High School, Palestine, writes some clever verse. He is author of more than one hundred poems, some of which have been used by readers in public entertainments. Here is one he has just penned, and the *Herald* is glad to give it space, not only because of its merit, but because it breathes a patriotic sentiment.

> Will you not bear a burden once
> For the red, the white, the blue –
> The symbol of democracy –
> Is it nothing to you?

It is to be regretted that C. F. Carr has ceased to produce.

The Encampment Choir

(Dedicated to the earnest efforts of Rev. L. L. Campbell of Austin, in establishing the encampment feature with St. John's Association. July, 1911.)

I hab been to many a meetin'
Whar much singin' was carried on,
Loud hosannas an' hallelujah's
From late at night 'til early morn,
I hab heard a thousand children
Wif their voices all well trained,
Singin' lake the heavenly choir
Comin' down de celestial main,
You hab nebber heard sich singin'
Dat could reach a sinner po'
Lak de singin' at de encampment
Dat I heard some nights ago.

Listen wif me while I tell you,
How it all did come about,
Den your soul will git right anxious –
Will hab to hold you, lest you shout,
Sittin' on a great big platform,
Square pianos, fiddles and horns –
You hab nebber heard sich singin'
Since de day dat you was born:
Fiddles, strings, and horns a-tunin'
To suit the music in the book,
Ha'ps and 'cordions all a-blowin' –
Made no diffunce whaih you look,

You could see some kind ob music.
Fittin' han's dat could slide an' pick,
Ef you listened for one minute
You'd git well ef you was sick.
Daih was Elder Campbell standin'

Bearin' time wid both his han's.
Sich a-singin' an' a-playin'
At de encampment – Goodness lan's.
It would make de angels listen
In the air w'en flyin' by,
Drive away all sins an' sorrows,
Make you t'ink your time was nigh.

Heah dat bass an' high soprano
Couplin' wif de strings an' notes,
Alto fittin' whar 'twas suited
Sweet enough for de heavenly host.
Ef you ebber felt your sorrows
Comin' down in heavy loads,
You jes' go to yonder hill-top
Whaih de folks am praisin' God:
Whaih de prayers for sinners searchin'
W'en you strayed 'way f'om de fold:
Sarches to de very bottom
Makes you drop your heavy load.

Did you say daih was no religion
Unless calm an' very still?
Your haid hab nebber been wet wif dew-drops
Lake de people on yonders hill.
You jes go an' sit an' listen,
Harden your heart, jes icy col':
Let your deeds and sins come double:
Hab no use for de shepherd's fold:
Den listen to dat choir a-singin',
Heah de words come loud an' full:
"Tho' your sins be red as scarlet
They shall be as white as wool."

Den your burdens will grow lighter
Wif de singin' of de choir,

Every now and den an "Amen"
Sets yo' soul on hallowed fiah,
Den see dat congregation standin'
Ez a hymn is given out,
Heah de words come f'om de preacher,
"Dark and stormy was de night".
Den de preacher, who was in earnest
'Bout de master's duty bound,
Raised it while the others followed –
You could heah it miles around.

Ez de sound through de air went floatin'
Echoin' through valley o'er dale an' hill,
You could feel de sperrit movin'
Overcoming your sinful will.
Ez it searched through every corner
Of your heart – once dead in sin –
Washing, cleansing, where it touches
Purifying de soul within.
You hab nebber heard sich singin'
An' perhaps you nebber will,
Lest you go and listen wif me
At de encampment on yonder hill.

(Not previously published.)

–Dedicated to the earnest efforts of Rev. L. L. Campbell of Austin, in establishing the encampment feature with St. John's Association. July, 1911

Malcolm Christian Conley

Malcolm Christian Conley was born in Burton, Washington County, Texas, one of the most thickly settled and cultured centers of Negro population in the state. He was educated in the public schools of Temple. Texas, and at Tuskegee Institute, Tuskegee. Alabama, where he was Class Poet of his class at graduation. He was the first Texas Negro to have his verse accepted and published by national periodicals.

Malcolm Christian Conley's verse has a tinge of mystery and at times of despair, while occasionally there are bursts of admiration for nature and praise of the beautiful. Now he is describing vividly some Biblical scene or happening: again he broods over dissatisfaction with life or love. But whatever he writes has the essence of the mystical, classical or devout. At the present time he is attempting to establish an art center at his home which will serve as a fitting abode for the cultivation of his artistic gifts.

For Mother in Paradise

I have washed you in my tears
    And have bleached you pure in dreams,
You, my comrade of the years,
    You, queen-opal of star gleams.
While I held you in firm grasp
    You slipped dreamily away:
But your passionate heart a clasp
    Left me holding 'til today.
I have tracked you on the sun
    Where the mist with flame has striven
To the music of the spheres,
    I shall trail you into heaven.

        (Not previously published.)

Four Walls

The world is my house of four walls:
    I tire of them.
Sometimes I rest my sight by looking
    Out of the window of dreams,
Upon the city of heaven.
Sometimes, in order to avoid gossiping company,
    I creep
Out of the back door called sleep.
    Some day
I'm going to throw my keys away,
And I'm going out of the front door
    To return no more.

        (Reprinted from *The Messenger*, April, 1930)

American Ideas

The red man looking upon rivers, plains, and seas,
Said, "Lord, let me hunt."
The white man looking thereupon
Said, "Lord, let me possess."
The black man, thereupon gazing,
Grew strangely fond
Of something vaguely beyond.
He with an open chest
Gave his heart a throbbing fling
Unto the glimmering mountain crest:
The stars his supplication hastened to ring
When he shouted aloud. "Lord, let me sing!"

(Reprinted from *The Crisis*, April, 1930.)

Lauretta Holman Gooden

Lauretta Holman Gooden was born in Sulphur Springs, Texas, where she attended school during her earlier years. Later her parents moved to Texarkana. She has always been interested in English literature and composition. She began writing verse at the age of ten and often amused herself and her friends by writing what she had to say to them in verse. Many of her first verses, while childish in sentiment, have beautiful rhythm and clarity of thought.

For many years Mrs. Gooden and her husband, John Gooden, have resided in Dallas, where they have operated successfully a grocery business. When asked what she regards as her greatest achievement. Mrs. Gooden smiles and says. "The rearing and educating of my deceased sisters children and my son."

Her verse is deeply emotional, intensely feminine, and vitally human. She is a lover of the out-of-doors and gives one through the medium of her well placed phraseology a vivid picture of life situations as impressed upon the heart of a woman.

A Dream of Revenge

Ah! How the wind raves this bitter night.
How the waters roar as they break upon the beach!
    Not a star is out.
Rave on, Winds –
Thunder on, Sea.
My heart beats time to the fierce music of your voices:
My heart feels the cold, maddened
Between the deeply suppressed conflicting passions
Of wounded love and outraged pride.

Ah! It suits me – this savage coast and water.
I like the howling chaos of wind and water:
A plan of vengeance comes to my darkened mind.
Yet why should I mourn the loss of love I never possessed?
What devil whispered vengeance to my soul?

The passionate tenderness is gone:
I plucked it from my heart as I would have torn a thorn from
    my flesh.
               (Not previously printed.)

Question to a Mob

O, cruel mob – destroying crew,
Who gave the life of man to you?
Why have you gathered, small and great,
To murder, more through sport than hate?

Do you not feel the pangs of shame?
When on your heads is placed the blame?
O, cruel mob – unpitying crew,
Who gave the life of man to you?

Has Heaven commanded you to take
Humans and burn them at the stake?
O, cruel mob – think what you do:
Who gave the life of man to you ?

O, fiends of earth that God gave breath,
Why do you love the sound of death?
What will you answer in Judgement? Who
Will say, God gave man's life to you?

                (Not previously published.)

RICHARD T. HAMILTON

Richard T. Hamilton was born in Montgomery, Alabama, March 31, 1869. He was educated in the public schools of that city and at Alabama State Normal School, from which institution he graduated in 1890 with valedictory honors. He taught in the elementary department of his Alma Mater but resigned to accept a clerkship in the Interior Department of the United States Government at Washington, District of Columbia, under the Civil Service. Later he matriculated in the Medical Department of Howard University, taking his M. D. degree in 1893.

Dr. Hamilton came to Dallas in the year 1901 and began practicing medicine. From the very outset he has, in spite of his lucrative practice, found time to give the welfare of his race deep study. He has given the public the benefit of this study from the platform and through the columns of the leading newspapers of the city and state. He is ex-president of the National Association of Life Insurance Medical Examiners. He has contributed verse and news articles to national magazines and newspapers over a period of years.

Sister Mandy Attends the Business League

Howdy, sister Mandy! Where you been t'nite,
    Looking kind o' thoughtful, looking kind o' bright?
I'se been to dat air meetin. dem bizness men dun had;
    I sure wood laff erbout it, if it wuzn 't kind er sad.
To hear dem talk erbout we ought to stick togedder,
    En patrinize our race men, insted er de udder:
When de man whuts doin' de talkin', en making er de speech,
    Don't do dat ting his self, don't practice whut he preach!

Now dare wuz dat doctor, whut spoke so loud n' long:
    He sed a heep er tings, dat wuz de truf, en strong,
'Bout our folks not sportin' dere own good bizines men,
    Who try ter be sumbody, en reely try ter win.
Honey, y'ought ter been dere! He sure knows how ter spout,
    I got so happy down dere, I longed fer room to shout!
But when I had de fever, whut makes you ake an' sore,
    Dis docter didn' sen' my med'cin' from no black man's store.
An' I wondered w'en he finished, er makin' dat air speech,
    Jes why he don't practice de gospel whut he preach.

An' dere wuz dat perfesser whut teaches in de school,
    He spoke so fine an' proper, er cordin to de rule:
But, I ain't no book larned 'oman, an' I don't understan',
    All de tings dats sed by er edicated man.
But when he wuz down las' summer, I showly do know,
    Dat wuz no cullud docter's car, er standin' at his do'!
En chile you shud uh herd our good ole preacher man:
    He burned us up er live as only preachers can.
'Bout havin' no race pride, en all dat sort er thing,
    An whut he sed dcee sure did hurt, it give er awful sting.
'Til I up an' membered, an' dat's de sad ole rub.
    De Dago store out dere by 'im, where he buys mos' all his grub!

So it wuz wid all dem biznes men at dat air meetin',
    Tellin' us pore folks whut ter do, it sholy wuz beatin,
Ter hear dem talkin' and er talkin', and er teachin'
    En none o' dem er practisin whut dey wuz up dere preachin'.
Dey thinks cause we pore folks ain't bin ter school,
    We air plum idiits, crazy, er jus' durn fools.
But we see everything, we ain't sleep, dey lead, we follow,
    En when we do lak dem, dey ain't got no right ter roller.
I bleves in race pride, but I ain't go throw no fit,
    When folks dos as I do, I ain't no hypocrite.
Yas sir, jes let dem talk all dey wants tuh, an' teach,
    But it's er goin in one car en out t'other, til dey
Practice whut dey preach.

    (Reprinted from *The Chicago Whip*, 1923)

A Negro's Prayer

Lord God of hosts, incline thine ear –
On bended knee we pray, make clear
What more must Africa's sons endure
For manhood rights – to have secure
The blessings of sweet liberty?
Lord God of hosts divine, to Thee
We meekly come, and plead, implore:
Oh God of all, what more, what more?

By force from Africa's shores we came,
We were enslaved, and in Thy name,
Oh God of all, were sold like chattel
Upon the auction block – dumb cattle,
Whipped and driven to till the soil –
(Oh years of unrequited toil)
Lashed and scourged till backs were sore!
Great God of hosts, what more, what more?

And then, oh Lord, oh God of might,
When days were dark, were black as night,
There came the call, as from afar,
"To arms, to arms, 'tis freedom's war!"
And in that bitter civil strife,
We gave our all – love, labor, life:
And still we're pressed, even as before –
Oh God so just, what more, what more?

We fought, Lord, that men might be free,
In distant lands across the sea:
For country, human rights and law,
We sacrificed in that great war:
But here at home and not abroad,
We are denied, oh God, our Lord,
An even chance. We're sick and sore!

Father of all, what more, what more?

Jeehovah, Lord, oh God divine,
We humbly pray thine ears incline –
We are oppressed, oh hear our plea!
We would like other men, be free.
Oh help us. Lord. Must we endure
Much more to have our rights secure?
Oh give us light, oh let us know
Lord God of all, what more, what more?

(Reprinted from the *Half Century Magazine*)

Maurine L. Jeffrey

Maurine L. Jeffrey was the only child of George and Reba Lawrence. She was born in Longview, Texas, October 16, 1900. Her parents moved to Dallas when she was three years of age. She attended the grammar schools of Dallas and was graduated from the J. P. Starks Elementary School. Her father died immediately after she completed her elementary school course and her mother then sent her to Prairie View College, where she studied for four years, completing the prescribed courses and making an excellent record. She was especially fond of history and English and has always been interested in music.

After finishing Prairie View, she taught school in the Dallas Public Schools for two and one-half years. At the end of this time she resigned her position to become the wife of Jesse W. Jeffrey, Jr., the eldest son of Professor and Mrs. J. W. Jeffrey. To this union two children were born: John Greer and Jessie Maurine. The latter lived only seven months. John Greer, the son, is at present a student of the Booker T. Washington High School at Dallas, Texas, and is a member of the school band. She began writing verse at an early age and produced some fine rhymes at the age of twelve. Her first published work appeared in 1924. She has been on the staff of several leading newspapers as a contributor in verse and has received favorable criticism from critics.

Maurine L. Jeffrey's verse is sentimental and contains much pathos. She has excellent descriptive powers and uses them well in many situations. She possesses the rare ability to be able at all times to give a true picture of the thing she wishes to portray. She shows in her writings the effect of a deeply religious and highly cultured environment, and seldom, if ever, does her verse escape this earmark.

My Rainy Day

I rather like old gloomy days,
When it seems the darkness will stay always,
When the rain falls pitter-patter on my pane,
It makes me recall my past again.

My mind goes back to my childhood days,
To brothers and sisters and childish ways,
I see Grandma getting the cookie jar
And Grandpa smoking an old cigar.

And even now, when the raindrops beat
Upon the roof, my day is complete:
For there's nothing that makes me half so gay
As the things that come with a rainy day.

(Reprinted from *The Dallas Express*)

Pappy's Last Song

Come heah, Liza, and set right down,
    Upon yo' ol' pappy's knee.
Carrie, draw dat chair around:
    I want you chillun to listen to me.

Heah, you Jimmy, set on dat flo',
    Sam, you set down on dat stool:
I ain't gonna tell you to keep still no mo':
    Look heah, boy, don't you dare act no fool.

Come heah, Ma. let dem pots and pans be –
    I know dem ole limbs mus' be tired:
But Lawd, you been so sweet to me,
    Pappy can't help feelin' 'spired.

Folks, I jes wanna tell you,
    Yo' ole pa's feeling mighty sad;
Clear your throats as you allus do,
    And sing a song to make pappy glad.

Raise dat hymn, Liza, daughter,
    As you do on Sunday morn:
Sing it soft, and slow, sorter;
    My 'ligion's a-risin', sho's you born.

Jimmy, son, drop in some bass,
    Sam, come on wit' a little tenor:
Ma, you lead dat s'prano in place,
    While Pa moans it like a sinner.

"Dere is rest fo' de weary,"
    Yes, yes, dat am true:
Oh, chillum, don't git dreary,
    Sing it on de whole night thoo.

An' if dis be's my last request,
    Yo' voices ringin' I'll heah no mo',
Lay ole Pappy's frame to rest,
    But keep on singin' soft and low.

Lillian Tucker Lewis

Lillian Tucker Lewis was born in Corsicana, Texas. She is a graduate of Prairie View College, and has done post graduate study at the University of Denver and at Kansas University. At one time she was an ardent member of the Priscilla Art Club, Ladies Reading Circle, and City Federation of Dallas. For more than fifteen years she taught school in the Dallas Public Schools. At present time she is a fraternal worker and Cashier-Bookkeeper for the Henderson Wren Funeral Home in Dallas.

Mrs. Lewis has always been interested in literature and dramatics. She has been writing creditable verse for a number of years, and was one of the first women of her race in the state to contribute verse to newspapers and magazines. A sympathetic attitude is displayed at all times in her verse with the man lower down, the unfortunate one. Her verse shows much precision. She uses deft skill in her portrayal of life situations. Her philosophy of life is revealed almost continuously in her verse, and is done in an exceptional manner. At times she is protesting vehemently against some practice of society, again she is in an optimistic mood, thrilled with thoughts of love past and present, and its possibilities. She feels life deeply and conveys to the reader through her verse the same feeling. This rare quality places her among the most mature in thought of the Negro writer in Texas today.

Longing

I never did
    Feel so blue
As when the day closed –
    And no sight of you.
Then when twilight began to fall
    I thought surely you'd come,
But you didn't at all.

I never did
    Feel so blue
As when they said you came –
    And I was gone.
I know that your love must have burned, too,
    And that you pouted, being alone:
But what could I do?

There is something about longing
    I can never relate:
'Tis like the breath of a rose,
    In a fragrant state.
Until the rose is held in hand –
    Then the petals droop
At God's command –

Becoming a memory
    As my longing is:
    Strange that such feeling
    Should bring one bliss.

        (Not previously published.)

J. Austin Love

J. Austin Love was born in Austin. Texas. As a child he was a dreamer and an ardent lover of nature. He had the rare opportunity of attending Tillotson College in Austin during the period when the president and faculty were white missionaries. Being subjected to this cultural environment, his native ability to write verse was strengthened and given impetus through the interest and instruction of his teachers. This is probably responsible for the beautiful and poignant lyrics he has written which place him far in advance of his contemporaries. He is perhaps the outstanding member of the group of verse-makers in his native state.

J. Austin Love's verse is smooth, rhythmical, and true to the life which he attempts to convey. It is local, yet universal in tone. The effect of rural influence is seen in most of his work. He is at present State Sunday School Director of the Holiness Church, and has written numerous hymns which are being used by the churches of his denomination.

Out in the Still, Wet Night

Out in the still, wet night,
    Where chirps the cricket and where croaks the toad
I hear the footsteps light
    Of someone passing down the lonely road:
I hear the gravel crash beneath two feet,
    I raise the shade, peering from left to right,
And still those footsteps fall with echoes fleet –
    Someone is passing in the still, wet night.

The rain drops on the roofs
    Which splash into the puddles on the ground,
Beat like the sound of hoofs
    Of frightened deer chased by the hunter's hound,
Still swells the sound of cricket and of toad,
    The moon bursts through a cloud and spreads its light,
I cast my eyes upon the rain-washed road
    And see one passing in the still, wet night.

With head hung slightly down,
    His body bent to turn the drenching rain,
Upon his face the frown
    That summons all one's strength some goal to gain,
I watch the figure slowly disappear,
    Then close the shade, extinguishing the light,
But still those crushing footsteps I can hear
    Go passing far, into the still, wet night.

        (Not previously published.)

Down Fish Trap Lane

Down Fish Trap Lane the trees begin to bud,
    The swallow and the bee are on the wing,
The cow stands in the shade and chews her cud
    The robin and the lark begin to sing,
Come, let us hasten through this furrowed field,
    Or cut across this patch of stubble cane
Still dotted with small shocks from last year's yield,
    Down Fish Trap Lane.
Down Fish Trap Lane, far down, beyond its end,
    The river slowly slides along its bed,
And in the deep holes where it turns the bend
    The lazy carp lies waiting, seldom fed,
Come, let us take our angle line and pole,
    Let's take our buckets and our minnow seine,
And spend an evening at the willow hole
    Down Fish Trap Lane.

(Reprinted from *Leisure Hour Lyrics*, 1922)

Joseph McMillan

Joseph McMillan was born in Marshall. Texas. He completed his work at Bishop College, where he received his A. B. degree. He later entered Kansas University and received his Master's Degree from this institution.

He has been principal of a school in St. Joseph, Mo., and is now Principal of the York Elementary School in Dallas. Joseph McMillan's verse is descriptive and usually has a touch of pathos, and sentimentality. Much of it borders on the psychic. He expresses his thoughts with vigor and forcefulness. He is one of the most brilliant scholars of the group.

Death Scene

The doctor turned away his head;
He felt the child would soon be dead.

The mother fled the dying room –
Her face was set with ghastly gloom.

And then she fell upon her knees
And troubled God with tearful pleas.

"That baby means so much to me.
Oh God, my God, how can it be?"

The doctor viewed the baby's face
And changed his mind about the case.

BIRDELLE WYCOFF RANSOM

Birdelle Wycoff Ransom was born in Beaumont, Texas, August 30, 1914. When she was four years old her family moved to Houston, where she later attended the Gregory Elementary School, and still later the Washington High School, from which she graduated as Salutatorian at the age of sixteen.

From 1931 to 1933 she attended the Houston Junior College, from which she graduated at the age of eighteen years, with valedictory honors. The following spring she began writing poetry for the Houston Informer under the heading "Lines of Life." She married at Galveston of the same year and discontinued this column some weeks later.

Birdelle Ransom speaks in the terms of race without mentioning race. Her verse portrays in a very vivid manner, race consciousness, which she weaves into her verse with accuracy and skill.

Night

Night, you are upon us:
We cannot know from whence descended,
Your infinite shade was manifest.
Immediately day had ended
We saw the gold up in the sky
And tinted clouds go sailing by:
We heard the wild birds' homeward cry:
Into your grandeur all were blended.

(Not previously published.)

J. C. Stevenson

J. C. Stevenson was born in Georgetown, Williamson County, Texas. His mother and father separated when he was just learning to walk. Because of the lack of support he only completed his elementary education.

He worked eight years as porter for the Kappa Alpha Fraternity at the University of Texas, in Austin. He afterwards entered the dining car service. For the past fifteen years he has been engaged in the tailoring, cleaning and pressing business in Austin, Texas.

Stevenson's verse shows that he has been a dose student of nature and that he draws on it for most of his subject material.

A Day's Recreation

Get away from your work.
Your office, for a day:
Get out in the open:
Where Nature's at play:
Get away from your task
Give your brains a rest,
Pull off that stiff collar,
That coat and that vest –
Take off those high heels,
Those transparent hose –
That paint off your cheeks,
Powder off your nose,
Gather up some tin cups,
An old frying pan:
Throw in a coffee pot
Or an old tomato can:
Get up real early
And begin to get busy.
Before the sun rises,
Be cranking up your Lizzy:
Go out on the river
Get under some trees
Where you can rest –
Get a whiff of fresh breeze,
Throw in your hook and line:
Forget about the blues:
Sprawl out on a grassy spot
And take yourself a snooze:
Leave off thinking
And deep concentration,
Enjoy for just once
A day's recreation.

G. T. Smith

G. T. Smith was born in Jennings County, Indiana. He came to Texas in 1891. He has written much verse and is still writing. In the year 1897 he won a $25.00 prize in a poetry contest conducted by the *Morning News*, a white daily of Dallas, Texas. The title of the poem was "Texas Independence." He speaks in an authentic and certain voice at all times. His best work has been done in dialect.

Watermelon

Watermelon in de night,
Shinin' in de pale moonlight
Right out in de sparklin' dew:
Tricks lak dat's not gwine ter do.
Great big melon on de groun',
Weighin' almos' forty poun's –
Right down whar de vines am thick –
Never heard uv sich a trick.
Nuffin' comes to earth to stay:
Ah's gwine take dat thing erway:
Take 'im off de col', col' groun',
Got 'im now – Ah's homeward bound,
When ah git nigh, wife's gwine say,
"Hubby comin' dis erway.
Look out boy – what dat you got?
Georgia Sweet? You sho am smart."
Den we'll carve 'im tuh de red –
Georgia Sweet, jes lak she said:
Nice red meat look lak pork chops:
Make our mouths go flip, flap, flop.
Den we'll carve 'im tuh de heart:
Th'ow dem two halves clean apart:
Wife take one-half – Ah take one –
Den de picnic's jes begun.
Hubby melons allus good:
Dis by 'sperience is understood:
Ah really think dis can't be beat,
Ah'm partial tuh de Georgia Sweet.
Dem great big hunks of nice red heart –
Eyes fly open – lips come apart:
Den de mouf comes open wide –
Juice uh runnin' down bof sides,
Chawnkin on a Georgia Sweet
Uh! Oh, chile, dat can't be beat.

(Not previously published.)

Lawrence Carlyle Tatum

Lawrence Carlyle Tatum was born on the Old David Farm at Avant Prairie, April 16th, 1893, in a small two-room log cabin. When he was four years old his parents moved to Mexia. He entered the Mexia public schools at the age of seven and attended school here for nine years. His father then sent him to Wiley College, Marshall. It was at the time of his graduation from the English Department of this college that he wrote his first poem, which was recited at the graduating exercises. After attending Wiley College for four years, he took the examination for a teacher's certificate and taught school for two years. Later he moved to Los Angeles, where he published two volumes of verse.

Lawrence Carlyle Tatum's verse rings true to life. His best work has been done in the form of lyrics and dialect verse. His dialect verse has a stronger appeal to the reader because of the fine manner in which he has portrayed characteristics of the Texas Negro. He has contributed to White dailies and Negro periodicals. He has been a cripple for twenty-two years, but this has not caused him to stop creating. He is married and has a son and daughter. He now resides in Mexia, Texas, where he is associated with government work.

Choicy

Talk er'bout yo' po'k chops
An' yo' I'ish stew:
'Bout yo' good ole beef roast
Simmahed thoo an' thoo:
Talk er'bout yo' chicken meat
Bein' sweet an' brown:
But gimme good ole 'possum,
Wid taters layin' 'round,

Take away yo' roun' steak,
Yo' tea-bone an' de lak,
Case dey isn't in it
When hit comes to nachul fac's,
Des gimme good ole 'possum
Wid de gravey oozin' out.
Is dat, you say, good eatin'?
Why, chile, dah ain't no doubt.

Dah ain't no use in 'scussin':
'Possum beats 'em all:
Even beats de cotton-tail
In de dead o' fall.
Ez fuh me, de things been settled,
Uh long, long time er go:
An' I'se ste'dfas' fixed on 'possum,
Ah don't want nuffin' mo'.

(Not previously published.)

BERNICE LOVE WIGGINS

Bernice Love Wiggins was born in Austin, Texas, March 4, 1897. Her mother died when she was five years old. After her mother's death she was carried to El Paso, Texas, where she lived with her aunt. During her high school career she created and recited her own verses. She is a graduate of the Douglass High School of El Paso, Texas. Under her supervision of one of her teachers, Miss A. L. McGowan, she was encouraged to rely upin herself in the writing of original rhymes. Her talent in versification is not surprising since her father, J. Austin Love, is himself one of the most outstanding Negro writers of verse in Texas and the Southwest.

Bernice Love Wiggins' verse has appeared in the *El Paso Herald*, *Chicago Defender*, *Houston Informer*, and the *Half Century Magazine*. Her best work is one in dialect and in this field she probably excels her contemporaries. A deep knowledge of the psychology of her people is portrayed through the medium of her dialect verse which at times rises to heights similar to those attained by the immortal Paul Lawrence Dunbar. Mrs. Wiggins now lives in Los Angeles, California. She is the author of a large volume of verse entitled "Tuneful Tales."

Church Folks

Good mo'nin' Sister Anderson:
How yo' cum on t'day?
Yo' aint cumplainin'? Well, dat's good,
I wish I felt dat way.
But I aint much. I'se all stov' up,
It's mos'ly in my knee:
I'se mighty 'fraid dat rumatiz
Is cumin bac' on me.
You wusnt out to meetin' Sunday,
Yo' say yo' couldn't go?
Well, dat's too bad, but den I 'low
Yo' didn't miss much do.

I'se t'inkin' whut a shame it 'tis
De way de chu'ch folks do:
'Taint many good ol' Christuns
In de chu'ch lac me an' you.
De chu'ch jus' full ob hypocrits,
Jus' 'tendin' lac dey's good:
Dey aint got no mo' 'ligun
Den whuts in dis piece ob wood.
De preacer he's so properish,
Dat I don't lac' him much –
But dat's de kind of man de hi'tones
Wants in our chu'ch.

Deres a mighty little 'ligun goin'
'Roun' now whuts wurf while,
Seem lac all de good ol' Christuns
Done laid down dey grace fo' style.
Yo' can sech de conjugation
Furn de pulpit to de bac',
An' won't fin' enuff pure 'ligun
Fo' to stop de smallest crac'.

Deres a heap ob so called Christuns
What jus' libs a life ob shame:
Why de sinners an' de chu'ch folks now
Is mighty nigh de same.

Deres Deacon Green – he's got a voice
Lac tom cats on a fence,
An' you wish dat he'd quit singin'
Furn de minit he commence.
He cums to chu'ch wid all his airs
Jus' mos' nigh dressed to deaf.
He oughter keep his mouf shet
'Count of licker on his breaf:
An' when dey calls on him to pray
He makes his prayer so long
To keep fum drappin off to sleep
I'se bliged to hum a song.

Dey got ol' Annie Johnson
Up dere singin' in de choir:
Now she caint sing an' know she caint
Den what is her desire
Fo' bein' up dere wid de res'?
De reason's plain to me –
She wears fin' clothes an' dere she sets
So all de folks kin see:
Tryin' to 'tend lac she so young
Dat 'oman's ole as sin
I 'spec' when I's a baby
She wus takin' comp'ny den.

Deres ole Miss Sildy's daughter
Jus' las' month she jined de chu 'ch,
An' las' week she give a break down ball
Yo' eber hear ob sech?
I know dat hits her bisness

But bac' dere in our day
Our Ma an' Pa'd a kilt us
Had we carried on dat way.
Hits a shame befo' de Master
How folks let dey younguns do
Taint many mudders raisin' up
Dey crops lac me an' you.

Ant Mary wus out las' Sunday
Now dat ole soul jus' aint right
Wearin' all dat store bought glory
On her head, aint she a sight?
Had it puffed all out an' twisted
Right in style, too, bless yo' soul:
Fixed up lac a gal ob sixteen
Hits a shame 'cause she's too ole.
Aint no sense fo' folks whuts her age
Over styles to rage an' rave
One foot in, de other ready
Fo' to slip right in de grave.

Yo' oughter seed ol' gran-pa Elec!
My, dat ol' man sho is spry:
Aint it awful? Why dat ol' soul's
Mighty nigh to ol' to die.
Talkin' 'bout he's gwine a marry
Soon as he kin fin' a wife.
How dese ol' folks cut sech capers
I caint see to save my life.
Course he's grown an' got a right
To do jus' as he please
Taint my bisness, but he oughter
Spen' mo' time upon his knees.

Folks so busy watchin' others
Dat dey aint got time to pray,

Goin' 'roun fum house to house
A gossipin' all day.
I don't talk about nobody
Sister, I aint got de time
Keeps de cross right on my shoulder
An' I hews right to de line:
I don't cast my lot wid sinners
An' I lives above all sin:
Course I takes a little toddy
Fo' my health's sake, now an' den.

I jus' don't b'lieve in talkin' 'bout
De way dat people do:
Dis little 'scussion whut we had
Is jus' 'tween me an' you,
But chile, de chu 'ch folks jus' aint right:
Mos' ob 'em's los' dey grace,
An' dere's a mighty heap ob dem
Won't see de Master's face.
I knows dat I'se a Christian, cause
My life is free fum sin:
I sho is sick dis mo'nin,
Has you got a little gin?

(Reprinted from *Tuneful Tales*, 1925)
El Paso, Texas.

–FIVE–
THE LIFE OF JOHN WESLEY ANDERSON IN VERSE

Dallas resident, Dr. J. W. Anderson, was a close friend of Brewer's, and for Anderson's seventy-seventh birthday (as well as his fiftieth year of medical service in Dallas) Brewer poetically provided Anderson with a biographical account of his life. Brewer admired Anderson, especially his commitment to helping the African American race in Texas and beyond. As Brewer noted, Anderson was among the nation's leading black philanthropists as well as a skilled and conscientious medical doctor. For more on Anderson see the article by Andy Galloway, "Anderson, John Wesley," in *Handbook of Texas Online* (http://www.tshaonline/org/handbook).

Originally published as J. Mason Brewer, *The Life of John Wesley Anderson in Verse*. Dallas, TX: Clyde C. Cockrell & Son, 1938. Reprinted by permission.

*****

DEDICATION
This volume is dedicated to John Wesley Anderson because of the many noble deeds for others, he has done.

ACKNOWLEDGMENTS
The Author wishes to express
The gratitude that's due
A good friend, Dr. John Lee Brooks
Professor at S. M. U.
The Author is also indebted
To a sister, Mrs. Gladys K. Miles,
For assistance in proof reading
Every once in awhile.

Preface

Since time immemorial
On rock, page, or scroll
What men have accomplished
Has always been told.

The service they have rendered,
The battles they have won,
The feats that they've accomplished.
The good things they have done.

So it is with great pleasure
I take pen in hand
To record the true story
Of a unique man.

A man who has prospered
And brought others health,
Who has shared with the public
Large sums of his wealth.

Unselfishly serving
His people, his age,
A learned Physician,
Philanthropist, Sage.

Doctor J. W. Anderson,
A man in first place
In helping and serving
His Maternal Race.

Cum Laude

'Tis only given to the few
To reach the halls of fame
And there inscribe in golden script
The letters of their name.

But he whose life is pictured
Within the pages here
Can walk into the Sacred Halls
Without trembling, or fear.

And take his pen and proudly write
"My name belongs in here."

The Office Building on Jackson Street
Where medicines he does mix
And interview his patients, was built
In the year eighteen-ninety-six.

The home adjoining the Office site
Showing a full front view,
Was erected twenty-six years later
In nineteen-twenty-two.

Birth and Childhood

The first day of September,
In eighteen-sixty-one,
At Lexington, Missouri,
To twain was born a son.

A fat and chubby little boy
With eyes of hazel blue
Brought joy into his mother's heart
And his grandmother's too.

His mother died when he had not
Yet reached the age of three,
And so the baby boy was robbed
Of her dear company.

Lest I forget a salient fact
As I proceed to write
The doctor like Frederick Douglass
Had a father who was white.

His grandma had to care for him,
And soothe his little heart,
And teach him things that she well knew
Would give him the right start.

He was born between two battles
During the Civil War,
For in July the Confederates took Lexington
But the time wasn't so far.

Before the Federal troops came
And captured the town again,
In a battle October the sixteenth;

So midst conflict, his life did begin.
An incident worthy of mention
On Curiosity
Was when five-year-old John Wesley
Put a bullet in a hole, in a tree.

He then set fire to the hollow tree.
And the bullet passed through the air;
And from this time on he's liked firearms
And of weapons has owned his share.

Years passed on and then the lad
When he was not yet eight
Was sent to live with an uncle
Into another state.

The state where he went was Kansas,
The town was Wyandotte,
And J. W. really loved
This pretty little spot.

He went to school there daily
Keeping his young life clean,
Excelling in his studies;
Was always good, not mean.

Medicine caught his youthful eye,
And Real Estate also;
He thought of these things all the time
No matter where he'd go.

As a youth he never worried
Financially, a day,
For dollars seemed to always get
Right in J. W.'s way.

From a very little fellow
He had home tasks to do,
But when Johnnie reached eleven
He hired himself out too.

Some other little boys and he
Who thought that work would pay,
Worked for a gardener ten hours
For twenty-five cents a day.

This occurred for the first time
In eighteen-seventy-two,
During the Summer, and gave him
Something worthwhile to do.

He earned twenty-five cents the first year
Per day, then thirty-five
For the second, and fifty, the third one,
But the fourth, for more he did strive.

So he got him another position
And worked in a nursery,
And made seventy-five cents daily,
So he made progress you see.

For from this time on the youngster
Paid his Room and Board
At his uncle's and auntie's residence,
And a few dollars did hoard.

So thus he became independent
Of others, at age fourteen,
And he's made his way ever since that time;
On no one has he leaned.

After working a year on this job
He changed his work once more,
And started cleaning sleeping cars,
His wages still did soar.

They paid him on this kind of job
Per month, the entire year,
Thirty-five dollars, so Johnnie's
Money was almost clear.

He labored at this for two years,
Kept the coaches clean
Until he finished the High School
When he was just sixteen.

The young John Wesley Anderson
At fourteen – who began
At this young age, to support himself,
As if he were a man.

While toiling for the Rail-Road folks
He studied his books some too,
For he had to be examined
To enter Kansas U.

They did not recognize the work
He did at Wyandotte,
So he had to prove to Kansas U.
He really knew a lot.

And this he did with his colors
Flying in the wind,
For when they saw his papers
They gladly let him in.

Early Manhood

He took his uncle as a sort
Of model to go by,
Because his uncle's ideals
Were all so very high.

His uncle belonged to the Council
Of the city of Wyandotte,
And the Board of Education too;
Of him, folks thought a lot.

Honesty and Industry
And punctuality
His uncle taught the alert lad,
Meant much as a degree.

And so the youth paid heed to this
And practiced what he'd learned
By putting to some worthwhile use
The money that he'd earned.

When he came back home from college
He made a nice long speech,
And they hired him where he went to school
In the same building, to teach.

They made him the First Assistant
The first year he was there,
And they paid him forty dollars
Which was doing pretty fair.

But the second year they made him
The Principal outright,
And moved to another building
On a lovely site.

They paid him sixty dollars then,
And the third year paid five more,
And moved the school another time
To help the children more.

While teaching, he was also
Studying with some men,
Some Doctors who taught the youth
Facts about Medicine

Encouraged by the Doctors,
In eighteen-eighty-three,
He quit to study Medicine
In Nashville, Tennessee .

The school was named Meharry
And right to day its name
Is synonymous with success,
With Medicine and fame.

For years it's served the Negro
By training Doctors Well;
Of all the Negro Doctors
Meharry Men excel.

So young J. W. entered here,
And as in days gone by
He led his classmates always
With averages real high.

His work was so outstanding.
Until he came to be
While still in school, a lecturer
Upon anatomy.

In Chemistry too, the youth,
Lectured from day to day,
And those who listened to him
Took down what he would say.

For he was versed in what he knew
Was thorough and profound;
One listening to the man could tell
For success he was bound.

John Wesley had invested
The money that he made
In Real Estate in Wyandotte
And it really paid.

For he made sufficient money
Out of his Real Estate
To pay his way through Meharry
From the beginning to closing date.

Having studied with Doctors at Wyandotte
Whose knowledge they let him share,
He only spent two years at Meharry,
Graduating with honors there.

He first settled down in Nashville
For two or three years or so
And then looked around for some place else
Better, to which he could go.

In thinking of a place to change
And practice medicine
His mind settled on Texas
Persuaded, by a friend.

He had a classmate at Nashville
Who put it in his mind
That down in Texas chances for
Good practice were real fine.

His uncle too had followed
The trail in his young days
From Missouri down to Texas
To Matagorda Bay.

So his uncle like his classmate
Thought that Texas was the place
For this young medic to settle
And to help himself and race.

Impressed by the talk of people
In eighteen-eighty-eight
He headed straight for Texas;
The grand old Lone Star State.

They'd told him of Gonzales
And other Texas towns,
But he chose from out the number
Dallas to settle down.

On Friday the thirteenth of July
In eighteen-eighty-eight
The young M. D. came to Dallas
And judged the place first rate.

He was not at all superstitious
Of Friday the thirteenth day
On which folks thought, if you started a thing
It would bring bad luck your way.

So he went and began his practice
That grew, and grew, and grew;
Because with all his patients
He knew just what to do.

The young man's fame spread far and wide
His success now was sure;
The slogan in Dallas became,
"See Anderson for cure."

They kept him busy day and night
Responding to some call;
He always had a pleasant smile
Not just for one, but all.

The nights never got too stormy,
The days never got too hot,
For this young and efficient Doctor
To go to a bedside, or cot.

To diagnose an illness,
Or ease an ache, or pain
Even though 'twas far past midnight.
In the midst, of a drenching rain.

Loyal to his patients all
He never turned them down,
And answered calls, even when
Snow was on the ground.

One night somebody called him
In a country town near-by
Stating that if he did not come
Perhaps the child would die.

So even though the night was cold;
A norther blowing strong;
He hurried out into the night,
And took a friend along.

The friend that he carried with him
Was known as Doctor Phipps,
A schoolmate of his at Meharry
Who went with him on night trips.

The child was saved from dying
And then he and his friend
Walked out into the cold, dark night
Met by a bowling wind.

They had no buggy and no horse
To take them back to town,
And the only way to catch the train
Would, be to flag it down.

So since they had no big red cloth
To wave forward and back
They built a red hot fire beside
The Katy rail-road track.

The plan worked fine for pretty soon
They, heard the engine blow,
And saw the headlight 'round the curve;
The train was moving slow.

The fire had served to flag it down
It stopped and they got on,
But they did not reach Dallas
'Til it was nearly dawn.

This incident is only one
Of many of the kind
In talking over Old Days
That cross the Doctor's mind.

Devotion to the folks he served
Came first with him always;
He sympathized with them in both
Their bright and dreary days.

And thus it was this Pioneer
In Medicine in the State
Came to be among the Rest
The one known as first rate.

With all the money that he made
And with his growing fame
He never changed his attitudes
They always staid the same.

And so by using common sense;
Investing wisely too;
His practice and his wealth each day
Just grew, and grew, and grew.

The Man and His Work

And now we come to Canto two
To sing a song of Praise
About the man and his fine work
He's done in many ways.

His great fame does not rest alone
Upon his work in Health,
Nor is it limited at all
By the status of his wealth.

There are other things that he has done
Along with his success
That have brought to hosts of people
Relief and Happiness.

Not only has he thought of self
As time has marched along;
He's also let his thoughts drift out
And settle on the throng.

In everything he thinks and does,
Included in the plan,
Somewhere, sometime or other,
Will be his fellow-man.

Unselfishness has characterized
His life throughout the years
He's laughed with those who're happy
And with the sad, shed tears.

A human being above all,
And not just a machine,
He's one of the noblest men who's lived
That folks have ever seen.

The Physician

Besides being a Physician
He's also a D.D.S.,
Having finished both at Meharry
Before he came to the Southwest.

He has also studied at Michigan
In eighteen-eighty-six
Believing that a Post Course there
Would put him in better fix.

To engage in his work as a Doctor
And properly diagnose
The cases that came before him
That would have puzzled most.

A constant thirst for knowledge
Obsessed this brilliant man
So in eigthteen-hundred and eighty-nine
He went to school again.

This time he went to Chicago
And entered Chicago U.
He put himself into his work
And excelled up there too.

The teachers all were so impressed
With his efficiency
Until the School awarded him
The degree D.N.T.

Doctor of Natural Therapeutics
Is what the letters mean
The Diploma's in his office
Right where it can be seen.

Not only has he Diplomas,
But on his wall you'll see,
A fellow of the American
Institute of Phrenology.

The only Negro member of
This Scholarly Concern
An honor that the honoree
Both deserved and earned.

For he was the valedictorian
Of the Phrenology Class
In the year of nineteen-hundred,
The others only passed.

Scholarships he's been given;
A lot of them – not just one,
And all of them have come to him
Because of what he's done.

No wonder then that his work ranks,
So very, very high
And that his Business grew by leaps
As years went gliding by.

Not only has he served his race
Their physical ills and needs,
But he has also doctored on
Those of other creeds.

Folks of other races too
Have sought his wise counsel
He's doctored on Mexican and White
And cured and made them well.

A doctor of the folks is he
Serving all who come,
Whether they hail from the group "Elite"
Or live in a dingy slum.

And so as a Doctor he is loved
By all who call him in;
They all acclaim him in accord
A Doctor and a friend.

His patients still keep him busy;
A thing to note with pride;
For it means that through the long, long, years
They've all been satisfied.

He's kept his hours promptly
And is in his Office Seat
Except when as designated
He takes time out to eat.

From eight to ten and twelve to one
He's there in the A. M.
And really between these hours
It's hard to contact him.

Because of the patients he has on hand
Waiting for their turn,
So about their illnesses, they
All will be able to learn.

And then in the afternoon again
He's there from three to five
Listening to the complaints of folks
Who want to be kept alive.

When evening rolls around he's there
From seven until nine
Writing Prescriptions and trying hard
To keep folks feeling fine.

And then when all the day's work's through
If someone rings the phone
He goes in response to the call
To ease some spell or groan.

He never yet has run across
A case that was too complex
For him to really fathom out
And give the proper text.

A thoroughly capable man is he
Well trained and sincere,
And in his field in the whole Southwest
He stands without a Peer.

Sidelights on Doctor and Mrs. Anderson

One on Doctor
Doctor claims that he has no favorites,
But I'm forced to think he's wrong,
For he buys many coca-colas
And drinks them all day long.

One on Mrs. Anderson
Mrs. Anderson would not dare admit
Her sentimentality,
But she's a great admirer of
The picture of a tree
That hangs on a wall in the Office,
Tinted in colors bold;
It's the tree she played 'neath as a little girl
In Louisiana, I'm told.

Another One on Doctor
One time he went to cash a check
From a customer out of town
And the Teller at the Bank asked him
If he knew any one around.

The Doctor looked at him and smiled
And asked him what he meant,
Stating that he didn't know clerks
But he knew the President.

Doctor Anderson at fifty-six,
At the height of his busy career,
Accumulating and ministering
To the sick, bringing them cheer.

Mrs. Anderson, just after she had arrived
Back in America, in thirty-five.

The Business Man

We've referred already to the fact
That he liked Real-Estate
Even when he was a youth, up in
Kansas, his uncle's state.

He had started while in Kansas
Investing in property some
Whenever the opportunity
For a bargain would come.

And so when he came to Texas
And started making good
He started buying Real-Estate
At the cheapest price he could.

He studied sites and locations
Building materials too;
And sometimes cut the price folks asked
For House and Lot in two.

He took notes on the building;
The direction it was in
So that when the purchase time came
He'd know just how to spend.

He had a natural gift it seemed
For knowing when to buy,
And this of course was always when
The price was low, not high.

In engineering Realty Deals
His knowledge was supreme;
As a man who knew property well
He was held in high esteem.

His appraisal of the values
And promises of land
As a real worthwhile investment
Were accurate and grand.

So consequently, year by year
His wealth always increased
And still his buying up of plots
Of ground never did cease.

Thousands and thousands of dollars
He's made because he knew
When it came to handling Real-Estate
Just when and how to do.

He knew the ins and outs of Law
And always read each fact
Before he placed his signature
Upon any contract.

His wealth soars up and onward
And agents are not lax
In figuring up per annum
The Doctor's Income Tax.

Although he never entered
A real Business School
He knows his Business Principles,
Each and every rule.

Not as a colored man, in business,
Is he hard to beat
But he will equally compare
With whites upon Main Street.

Banker, Clothier, Jeweler, All,
Whatever they may be,
Have not done more with what they've earned,
Or spent wiser, than he.

He never hurries into Deals
He always takes his time
To make sure that in trading
He will not lose a dime.

He takes peeps into the future,
Looks well into to-day,
And then surmises whether
Or not the thing will pay.

If he thinks the deal's a good one
He signs the dotted line,
But if he judges otherwise
He just says, "I decline".

And so it is this wizard of
Financing stands ahead
Of Business men among his race
The living and the dead.

The Philanthropist

Like all great men who are truly great
He looked around to see
How he could best share what he had
With Humanity.

So first of all in thinking
About what he should do
His mind went back to Meharry
Where he'd learned the things he knew.

Inspired by the thoughts of his college,
Events he could recall;
He gave to it, twelve thousand dollars
To erect an Anatomical Hall.

The school named the building "Anderson"
After the donor of
The money to finance its erection
Because of his loyal love.

The reason he gave them the building
The campus to adorn
Was because the dissecting room formerly
Was over a rickety barn.

He was not contented with this though
He wanted to keep on
Doing things for the common good,
So new ideas were born.

Into the fertile mind he had
To do more things worthwhile
That would help his fellow-creatures,
And make all of them smile.

For long years he had lived near-by
The White Y.M.C.A.
And he became impressed with boys
Who passed that way each day.

Somehow these youths were different
From others of their race,
So Doctor Anderson noticed this
When they'd stop by his place.

They often came to talk with him,
Telling him what they'd done
That evening at the Y.M.C.A.
The things they'd learned – the fun.

So when they had a big campaign
To build a Negro "Y"
In Dallas, for its colored youth,
And excitement ran high.

The Doctor became interested
In giving it a start
So he put ten thousand dollars
In it for his part.

Because he felt that if it helped
White boys be better men,
It could do the same for colored,
And he put his money in.

Year after year since this first day
He helped to build the "Y".
His donations to the Moorland Branch
Have been constant and high.

He's given memberships to boys
At the Moorland "Y".
And many dollars in Special Drives
As the years passed by.

'Til now at the present time the count
Of his gifts up to date
Totals more than eighteen thousand
To nineteen-thirty-eight.

Thinking that what was good for young men
Was good for woman-kind,
He gave large sums to the Y.M.C.A.
To help girls be refined.

Another thing that impressed him most
About the Y.M.C.A.
Was that it was non-denominational,
Treating all the self-same way.

His interest then turned to Churches;
He gave of his means to them,
And helped do more with his dollars and cents
Than the members who lead the hymns:

Then Orphan Homes and Hospitals
Came in for their share
Of the gifts that he was distributing
Ofttimes, here and there.

He did not confine his allocations
Just to causes that were black,
But in the distribution of
His funds, he used good tact.

Impressed by the very fine spirit
Of the White Freeman's Hospital in town,
Where they look after children of all races,
Never turning one down.

To the proposed Texas Children's Hospital,
Because Freeman's was fair,
He donated one thousand dollars
To help it with child care.

He's a most loyal citizen of Dallas,
His interest is concrete,
For he paid six thousand two hundred-forty dollars
To help open St. Paul Street.

This amount was his part for the opening
Of the block leading to Commerce;
And of all the property owners
He paid his money first.

To the Dixon's Orphanage at Gilmer
He gave large sums each year,
Amounting to thousands of dollars
To bring the Orphans cheer.

Then College and High School education
Attracted his active eye,
And he thought for these Institutions
To do something he would try.

So he started right into his giving
To Wiley, St. Peters and all,
And his name in these schools became legend
Throughout the college halls.

Then came a call from the High School in Dallas
For books to study in,
A new course in Negro History
That they were to begin.

After thinking it over for several days
Doctor Anderson said, "Yes,"
And wrote them a check for two hundred books
To the Associated Negro Press.

And then a graduate of Washington High School
Whose average was ninety per cent,
Who had no one to send him to college,
For four long years was sent –

To Wiley College where he finished up
And took his A.B. degree.
The boy in question is Albert Williams
Who has proven himself to be –

Worthy of the money the Doctor spent
In giving him a chance
To go and complete his college work
So he could advance.

Then recently when the High School wrote
Its history up in prose,
Doctor Anderson gave more than the rest
The list of donors shows.

He's the greatest of race Benefactors
On the Western Hemisphere,
For his gifts totaling fifty thousand
Cannot be exceeded here –

By any Negro on the continent,
Nor in the Isles of the Sea
He's the greatest this country's afforded
And perhaps will always be.

We could even go a step further,
And might be right if we'd say
That he's the world's leading Negro Philanthropist
Up to the present day.

Home Life

When we read of men's triumphs and failures
It's well to bear in mind
That in either one of these instances,
Involved is woman-kind.

The heights to which men ascend often
Are not reached by them alone,
But with the aid of a helpful companion
That they can call their own.

While the thoughts, acts, and deeds of our Hero
To his native gifts are due,
His wife, Mrs. Pearl Carina Anderson,
Comes in for her part of it too.

They were wed in the month of October,
The tenth day, nineteen-twenty-nine,
In the city of Kansas City, Kansas,
To each other themselves they did bind.

And there has been no happier Union,
From what this scribe can see,
Than exists between these two people
In marriage history.

The finest relationships always
There are between he and she,
There may be a happier couple
But I don't see how there could be.

For they are constantly with each other
Throughout the day and night.
If you look up and see one of them
You'll know that the other's in sight.

For they are really and truly interested
In each other's welfare.
And when problems and projects confront them
Exchange of opinions they share –

And usually when they have expressed them,
They always soon agree
On a procedure in the situation,
That is satisfactory.

She's a real help-mate and a housewife;
She helps with the office chores,
Even down to greeting the patients
Who enter the office doors.

Thoroughly absorbed is she in her husband's work,
She's always at his side,
In the way he cares for those who're sick
She takes a deal of pride.

She's constantly moving to and fro,
Helping where she can;
Even if it's just a pencil, that
She puts in her husband's hand.

She's careful about his diet too,
Looks after the physical man,
And makes, him partake very strictly always
Of the things in the menu plan.

His hours of rest are religiously watched,
He cannot be disturbed at all,
For his faithful and vigilant companion
Answers each telephone call.

When the work of the day is all over
They may go out for a ride,
Or get them a paper or good book to read
And remain together inside.

When considering an investment
He never makes a move
Without first calling in Mrs. Anderson,
To see if she will approve.

In their home are beautiful paintings
Hung high in Marble Halls,
And scattered throughout the mansion
Upon pretentious walls.

Patrons of Art are both of them,
Lovers of beauty too;
Their interest in cultural-aesthetic things
Is only excelled by few.

They work harmoniously as all folks should
When they have been made one,
Considerate of each other's every wish
Daily, from sun to sun.

They're a perfect couple though bound in an age
When married life is queer,
But their marriage-ship is the pride of the fleet,
For it's made the harbor clear.

The Doctor's great loyalty to Texas
Is portrayed in his Oil Paintings fine;
"Summer in Texas", and "Bluebonnets" too.
Are titles I have in mind.

These Paintings, and others, adorn his walls
And beautify his place.
"Nook in White Rock Lake" and "Breckenridge Park"
Also occupy space.

Most all of his Pictures are of Texas
Landscapes in a definite spot.
So it's easy to tell by his Paintings
Whether he's faithful or not.

For no one compelled him to purchase
Any particular one,
He just thought of his state of adoption
Whenever the buying was done.

And instead of buying some Picture
Of another state, or land,
He selected from all that were shown him
Those with a Texas brand.

Miss Ruth Anderson, the daughter,
A young and talented Miss,
After finishing up at St. Peters,
Went and got on Xavier's list.

But Romance came an entered
Into her youthful life,
And she became after four months
A fine young man's dear wife.

The young man hailed from New Orleans
A prominent family there,
Of French descent named Dejoie
So the match was rather rare.

Country Home

Having lived as a boy in the country
And breathed its fresh morning air,
He decided to build him a Country Home,
As his mind wandered way back there.

He remembered how wholesome and healthy
Most all country people are;
So he thought he would buy him a plot of ground
That wasn't so very far –

From the hum and drum of the city's wheels
Where he could rest when he pleased
And enjoy the beautiful landscape views
And gaze at majestic trees.

So he started to look around about
For a site that would be best,
'Til he found sixteen acres of ground
Running East and West –

On the paved highway of Forest Lane,
Ten miles North-west of town,
So he went and saw the owners
And laid his money down.

Its eastern boundary is White Rock creek
For eighteen hundred feet;
And the scenic views along this stream
With any will compete.

Whether they're scenes from the Rockies
Or from some foreign land,
None of them are more picturesque
Nor can they be more grand.

A gurgling branch with a lovely spring,
A creek that never goes dry,
With beautiful trees along its banks,
And cliffs towering high.

To the North and higher, is a great big farm
Where sediment washes down,
And leaves its rich alluvial deposits
On Doctor Anderson's ground.

Thus he's furnished rich fertilizer
For all his gardening,
Enriching the land that he cultivates,
Without costing him a thing.

Next to the Highway is a gravel bed,
Each rain brings gravel this way,
So all of the gravel that's used for the Drives
Is provided the place without pay.

The strip of land first was a thicket
With no improvements – not one;
So the Doctor established a home there
In June nineteen-thirty-one.

He first built Casita del Campo,
A brick home with roof of tile,
And added a caretaker's cottage
After a little while.

A six-thousand gallon water tank
Was erected later on;
From the clouds, a well, and a nearby spring
Its supply of water is drawn.

A garage, where the tractors and trailers are kept,
As well as a huge lawn mower,
Is used for various purposes
Like keeping things in store.

A permanent kitchen and barbecue pit
Are on the boys' camp ground;
The kitchen's a replica of a log cabin
Stained a walnut brown.

The barbecue pit's the best of its kind,
Modern and up-to-date,
Combining all of the fine features that
Have just come out of late.

The place has been changed totally,
From thicket to modern abode,
With enchanting graveled Driveways
Replacing the old-time road.

Grass has been planted and flowers
And concrete walks put down
Around the Peninsula that is formed,
As Buffalo Branch winds round.

There are also concrete steps that lead
Down where the "Y" boys swim;
They were put there just purposely
To accommodate them.

There's also another set of steps
On the edge of White Rock creek,
And boys may clamber down them, when
Some fish they wish to seek.

Water is brought from a neighbor's spring
In a pipeline across the creek,
Through a hundred and seventy-five feet of piping
That hasn't a single leak.

From a part of the one and some acres
Of land that he had in cane
He got forty-four bales of rich mellow hay
In spite of scanty rain.

There are four well-built, strong, iron bridges
Beneath which Buffalo Branch flows;
Two of them are used by pedestrians,
And two over which traffic goes.

Tomatoes, cabbage, and onions are raised
On the garden spot,
And occasionally other plant life too
Upon this little plot.

There's a cow here and some chickens too,
As well as two fine dogs,
Called Duke and Tassel, respectively
Who chase the squirrels over logs.

Elm, Pecan, Ash, and Oak trees stand.
Symmetrically arrayed,
As if they were giant Cossack soldiers
Going on parade.

Tall and stately of bearing they are,
Clothed in robes of green,
With circling, meandering Driveways
Wending their way between.

As you leave the Highway and enter the gate
You take "Creek Drive" to the right
Where "White Rock Creek" with its entrancing views
Brings you sheer delight.

And then to "Ridgeway Drive" you proceed,
Trees swaying in the breeze,
Where mocking birds and red birds too
Are chirping melodies.

Within sound range of "Lover's Lane Drive"
They sing their joyous songs,
And your heart is filled with ecstacy
As you drive along.

There is "Buffalo Drive", and "Central Drive", too,
That are lined with foliage,
So beautiful until I cannot find words
To describe them on this page.

And Casita Del Campo – how
Can I picture the place?
It means little house in the country,
And it is truly an Ace.

There are two day-beds in the Living Room,
An antique clothing rack,
A rustic clothes closet in a corner there,
Some curtains that fold back.

In the Dining Room is a table round,
Paintings of food and fruit,
And you get a view of "Buffalo Drive"
Looking East, to boot.

In the kitchen's a cook stove and cabinet
And wood to start a fire;
So you see that Casita Del Campo
Has all one would desire –

To make him contented and happy
And enjoy the things of life;
And that's exactly what it's doing
For the Doctor and his wife.

Every morning at precisely five-thirty
The Doctor gets up and goes
Out to this most gorgeous estate
To get joy and repose.

And now for the most important strong link
in the entire Country Place Chain,
We come to the fine highly cultured young man
In whose care it's left in the main.

He is Weldon K. Groves – hails from Kansas.
He's the Doctor's cousin too,
And no greater young fellow than he is
Ever entered Kansas U.

He spent three years at the school there,
Acquitted himself valiantly,
But decided at the end of this period
A doctor he didn't want to be.

He's as proud of the place as its owners are,
Taking things in hand,
And always carrying the activities out
Just as the Doctor planned.

This is the place that the Doctor bought,
Not just a foolish whim,
But as a recreational center
For the patients who came to him.

So that when they were convalescing
And were able to get about,
They could loiter here and regain their strength
And get healthy and stout.

Not only did he think of the sick folks,
But he thought that it would pay
To permit churches, schools, women's clubs and the like
To have picnics there, night or day.

Without making them any charges at all,
Simply that they act right,
And leave the grounds clean like they found them
And not in a sorry plight.

Desiring to enlarge the services
Of this lovely spot
He let the Y.M.C.A. have a Summer Camp here
To improve the youngsters' lot.

For two summers now Mr. Howell,
Boys' work secretary of the Y.M.C.A.,
Has directed a one-month Summer Camp,
Religion, Education, and Play.

Friendships and Testimonials

The friendships he's formed are numerous,
Some far away and some near;
But wherever they are they are lasting
And genuinely sincere.

He numbers among his fine friendships
Many men of National fame,
But he treats those of lesser standing
And the more prominent ones, the same.

As the Doctor is to the friends he has,
So are the friends to him;
They all regard this wonderful man
As a precious human gem.

We cannot jot down here the statements of all
About him as a friend,
But we'll list a few that the oldest of
His many friends have penned.

We'll first take the W. W. Maxwells
And record what they think
Of his fifty years of friendship
Without a broken link.

"A man as true as steel", they say,
"Who does things that mean most",
"Whose high type thought and dignity
Are things of which we boast".

Dr. S. W. Armstrong an old friend
Of fifty years and more
States that the doctor's friendship
Is the best he has in store.

He's never in his entire life
Had a friend as good
Nor one so worthy of tribute
As to fine manhood.

And then Channing H. Tobias
Head of the Y.M.C.A
For Colored youth throughout the world
Has these words to say.

Doctor Anderson's loyalty to Y. Work
Has been an inspiration
To the Association Brotherhood
Throughout the entire nation.

Next in line comes R. B. De Frantz
National councilman
And personnel man of the colored work
In this and other lands.

He says the impressive example
Of the doctor's giving has been
The deciding factor that makes him
One of our country's great men.

Doctor Dogan of Wiley College,
Its veteran President,
Himself of National prowess
Lists what the doctor's meant.

"You have been unselfishly brotherly
Very anxious that the best
Come to all those who are deserving
Of Honor and Success."

Doctor Turner of Meharry college,
Its recent President-elect,
Expresses the Doctor's service to all
In statements firm – correct.

"Doctor Anderson's inherent gifts and
His benefactions too
To both local arid national problems
Is paralleled by few."

Mr. J. H. Henry, Secretary of
The White Y.M.C.A.
In Dallas, and a former State "Y" Head,
Has these nice things to say:

Dr. J. W. Anderson's a man of "firsts",
A thinker who achieves,
Always constructive in his acts,
Stands by what he believes.

Constantly putting the best he has
Into his every deed,
And expecting others that he works with
To follow this worthy creed.

Steady of counsel this wizard is,
Far seeing in his way,
Knowing that only when one puts in
An account, does it ever pay.

Looking down through the cracks in the floor
Of an old carriage room
In a dissecting class at Meharry,
Great thoughts in his mind did loom.

"When I start to practicing medicine",
This purposeful young man said,
"I will give this college a building
Where they may dissect the dead".

Doctor Anderson's cash contribution
To the Moorland Y.M.C.A.
Is the largest amount in the entire world
For a Negro citizen to pay.

He has also made gifts to the National
And State "Y" Setups too,
And he hasn't stopped yet in his giving;
He still continues to do.

These friendship remarks and statements
From folks all go to show
The rare type that his service is
To the high, as well as the low.

Travel

Both the Doctor and wife are travelers
Taking vacations each year,
Sometimes to far distant countries
And often to spots that are near.

He likes the lower Americas
Haiti, Cuba, Panama,
And in talking about his voyages
Tells clearly what he saw.

In eighteen-ninety-three he went
Into Old Mexico,
And in nineteen-and-thirty-three
To Santo Domingo.

He also went to Haiti then
To learn more of his race
Because he'd heard John M. Langston
Years back, describe the place.

The Doctor likes the Western world
But Mrs. likes the East,
So in nineteen-hundred-thirty-five
She had her Travel Feast.

The Doctor left it up to her
The route she wished to choose
So she forthwith decided on
A Mediterranean cruise.

Taking in the countries that
Bordered on this sea
From Spain to Asia Minor,
Through France and Italy.

To Africa too she journeyed,
Way down in Egypt's land,

For the African Coast was listed
In her travel plan.

The trip lasted for three long months,
Embracing many climes,
Most of them warm and balmy
But some of them cool at times.

Resume

When Doctor Anderson came to Dallas
There were thirty-thousand here
But now it has reached three-sixty
In a period of fifty years.

He has seen just twenty-three Doctors
And Dentists come and go
Since he came here and hung out his shingle
Fifty years ago.

Of his many distinctions and honors
One that he likes best
Is the honor of having delivered
The first graduating address.

To the first Dallas High School Graduates
In eighteen-ninety-two
He regards this as one of the finest things
That a man could do.

He's been helping the Free Schools of Dallas
Ever since that time
And has given the schools and the children
Many a dollar and dime.

Every man or woman who has ever
Worked for the Doctor some
Has caught the fine spirit of thrift he has
And bought themselves a home.

His contributions to Civic growth
And also to race progress
Rank him with those who have nobly served
And who have achieved success.

A remarkable thing about his life
Is that he can truly say
That during fifty years of practice
His office has not closed a day.

Even though he was disabled
Or taking time off for a space,
He had his office open
And someone to take his place.

He's been filling his own Prescriptions
Since nineteen and seven, too,
And in this span of years his patients amount
To seventy thousand, three hundred-thirty-two.

He's a man of wit and humor
As jovial as can be;
No one can enjoy or tell a joke
And like it more than he.

Larger and larger the leaping flame
Of his achievement grows;
Brighter and brighter the bonfire of
His Philanthropy glows.

A dinner and Testimonial
On the last thirteenth of July
Was given by friends in his honor
Down at the Moorland Branch Y.

An interesting Program was rendered
Lauding the honoree
For the useful life that he had lived
In his community.

One took him as a Pioneer
Others another phase
Of the Doctor's very successful life
And each one gave him praise.

But he only got what he deserved
For there is no one anywhere
Who is more entitled to words of Praise
Than he is to his share.

The good that he's done for his brothers
Will live forevermore
And, assure him a real safe journey
From here to the other shore.

He won't have to knock when he gets there
And tell St. Peter his name,
For preceding his advent to Heaven
Will be his work and his fame.

Thus is the Hero we have pictured
Not for the battles he's won
But for the hundreds of good things
For others he has done.

To Dr. Anderson
My dear and honorable Doctor:
I am grateful as can be
To you, for letting me write in verse
Your colorful history.

To All of You
And now we have finally come to the end;
I hope you've enjoyed the lines that I've penned.

—J. Mason Brewer

A Toast to Dr. J. W. Anderson
On His Seventy-seventh Birthday
September First, Nineteen-Thirty-Eight

No one knows like the Doctor knows
The joy and happiness
That have come to him when he has helped
Some brother in distress.

No one knows like the Doctor knows
What pride and ecstasy
Have come to him when he's cured for good
Some patient's misery.

But we all know and we ought to know
How great his work has been
Since seventy-seven years ago
When his life was ushered in.

A toast to him then, a loud Hurrah!
For his Philanthropic ways,
That have caused him to give so lavishly;
A million shouts of praise!

Forecast

The story's told but not in full,
His work is not done yet.
There are other tasks he must perform
Before his Sun has set.

--SIX--
JOHN TALES

As Modie C. Boatright noted in his introduction to J. Mason Brewer's folklore collection of "John Tales," Brewer's ability and effort as a folklorist was being recognized nationally as well as in Texas. Boatright pointed out that "John Tales are part of the lore collected by J. Mason Brewer on a General Education Board Grant sponsored by the Texas Folk-Lore Society in 1937-8. They are added to an increasing list of significant contributions to American Negro folk records." John is the trickster hero of the southern plantation. John always comes out victorious in his contests with the slave owner or overseer. As a result John is a general folk hero symbolizing an entire group. Other folk heroes were real, and many stories were told about them also, including such African Americans as Huddie "Leadbelly" Ledbetter, Harriet Tubman, and Jim Beckwourth.

Originally published as J. Mason Brewer, "John Tales," *Mexican Border Ballads and Other Lore*, edited by Modie C. Boatright. Austin: Texas Folklore Society, 1946. Pp. 81-104. Reprinted by permission of the Texas Folklore Society; thanks Kenneth L. Untiedt.

*****

How the Boss-man Found Out John Was Taking His Chickens

Colonel Clemons thought that chicken was too good for plantation hands to eat, so he would never let his hands eat one. The only kind of meat he would let them have was dry salt bacon from his commissary, and the only kind of wild game he allowed them to eat was possum. If he caught a hand with a chicken, he would punish him. For this reason the poor field hands very seldom had chicken for dinner. Now and then they would take a nice fat hen off the Colonel's chicken roost, but they had to slip out and cook it, because Colonel Clemons was always coming down to their cabins at meal times and looking at the food on their tables. If he saw any kind of meat except salt bacon or possum, he would take it and throw it out of the cabin door on the ground.

Most of the hands on the plantation had got to the place where they were afraid to take any more chickens, but John wasn't. Every Saturday night he went to Colonel Clemons' chicken roost and took two fat hens for his Sunday dinner.

The Colonel would always miss his chickens but he never could catch the thief. He felt somehow that it must be John; so one Sunday about twelve o'clock he walked down to John's cabin. When he went in, the first thing that attracted his attention was the odor of some kind of meat cooking.

"What's that cooking, John?" said the Colonel.

"Possum, boss, possum," replied John.

"I've been hearing about what a good possum cook Mariah is," said the Colonel, "'so I think I'll stay here and sample some of her cooking."

"Sho, boss, sho," replied John. "Takes long time to cook possum good."

So the Colonel stayed another half an hour. Still Mariah didn't serve dinner. The Colonel got up from the stool, walked over to John and said, "John, looks like to me that possum ought to be done by now; I'm going over there and see about him myself."

And with these words the Colonel walked over to the fire place where the meat was cooking and pulled the lid off the pot. Instead of the possum he saw two of his fattest hens.

"John, you thievin' rascal," he said, "these aren't possums, they're chickens."

"Says dey is, Boss, says dey is," replied John. "Well, dey wuz possums when Ah put 'em in dere, if dey's chickens now Ah'm gonna th'ow 'em away."

JOHN AND HIS BOSS-MAN'S WATERMELON PATCH

Some of the plantation owners in the neighborhood gave their hands an acre of land to raise vegetables, corn and watermelons on, but Colonel Clemons was so mean that he would not let John and the other hands raise any food at all for themselves. He wanted them to buy everything at his commissary.

So it was hard for Colonel Clemons's hands to get a watermelon even in watermelon season. He wouldn't let them have any from his own patch, and he wouldn't give them any money to buy them from other plantations. So John secretly visited the Colonel's patch once or twice a week and took several watermelons home. David and Joseph, his little boys, always went with him and helped him bring them down to the cabin.

This had been going on for three years now and the Colonel hadn't caught up with them. But one Saturday evening when he was returning from town, he saw John and the little boys leaving his watermelon patch. Each had a mellon on each shoulder. The Colonel rode up to them and stopped his horse.

"I've been missing a lot of watermelons out of my patch lately," he said to John. "Lots of tracks lead up this way, and it seems like those watermelons you have may be mine, you thievin' rascal."

"Things ain't always what dey seems, Boss," replied John.

"Well," said the Colonel, "you are coming from the direction of my patch."

"What direction go to do wid a hones' man?" answered John.

The Colonel was so outdone with John's reply that he headed his horse toward the big house and went on home.

How John Learned to Count

Besides his work in the fields, John fed the hogs and other stock on the plantation. The Colonel often scolded him for not being able to count the hogs in the pigpen each evening when he went to feed them. Every time the Colonel would ask John how many hogs there were in the pen, John would say, "Dey's all here, boss." This made the Colonel very angry and he threatened to whip John if he did not learn to count the pigs. So John, not wanting to have trouble with the Colonel, decided he had better learn to count.

Looking down towards the Colonel's house one evening, he saw the Colonel's little nine-year-old grandson playing out in the yard; so he called him and asked him to count the hogs for him. The little boy came and counted them. The next evening when the Colonel came down to the pen, he asked John how many hogs were there. "Dey's all here boss," replied John, as always. When John said this the Colonel got angry as usual and told him that he'd better know how to count them tomorrow evening.

"Sho, sho, boss," said John, "Ah bet yuh five dollars Ah kin count 'em tomorrow evenin'."

"All right," said the Colonel, "that's a bet."

The next evening when the Colonel came down to the pen he asked as usual, "John, how many hogs are in the pen?" The little boy had told John that there were eight hogs in the pen, and had taught him how to count them, but John was so excited about winning the five dollars from the Colonel that he had forgotten all about adding; so he answered in a hurry, "Dis one an' dat one, an' dat one an' dis one, de ol' black sow, two more an' another one."

John and the Butting Sheep

One year turkeys were very scarce on the plantation, so Colonel Clemons told John to kill two sheep for Thanksgiving dinner in the Big House. John's family had never tasted mutton, because the Colonel would not allow them to eat it, but John secretly took a chunk of meat and carried it home so Mariah could cook it for their Thanksgiving dinner. John, Mariah, and the little boys enjoyed it so much that they were just crazy for some more. But they did not want to wait until the next Thanksgiving day, and it wasn't likely that the Colonel would kill another sheep before that time. John decided that the only way to get mutton was to steal a sheep.

He knew that this was risky business so he kept putting it off, but one night his craving for mutton got the best of his fear of the Colonel, and so he armed himself with a hickory club and slipped down to the sheep pen. When John entered the pen, a sheep started to his feet. John knocked it in the head. Just as he was about to hit a second sheep, he heard footsteps approaching. When he looked up he saw someone coming up to the pen. It was Colonel Clemons. John yelled as loudly as he could, "Ah ain't gonna let no daw-gone sheep butt me to death."

John as a Coachman and the Rats

Occasionally on Sunday afternoons John drove the Boss-man and his family over to the Boss-man's brother's plantation, in the coach. Since these visits usually lasted three or four hours, John always grew tired of waiting, but the Colonel gave him orders not to get down off the driver's seat for fear the horses would run away. Sometimes he would get so sleepy that he could hardly keep his eyes open.

One summer the Colonel got to visiting his brother twice a week, and each time John would get sleepier and sleepier. He finally decided to disobey the Colonel and find himself a place to lie down. Fortunately his little boys, David and Joseph, always went with him and played with the duck and guineas in the barnyard. So John found him a place to rest and got the little boys to watch for the Colonel's return. He told them to wake him up when they saw the Colonel start out of the house.

John went to a large haystack not for from the place where he slopped the coach and lay down and went to sleep.

Now the Colonel usually stayed three or four hours, but this day David and Joseph were fooled, because he stayed only one hour. The Colonel had come out of the house and had almost reached the coach before they saw him. In a big hurry, they shook John, woke him up, and told him the Colonel was coming. John got up, half asleep and half awake and started running toward the coach at full speed.

"What are you doing off that seat, John?" said the Colonel.

"Catchin' rats, Boss, catchin' rats," replied John.

"How many you caught?" asked the Colonel.

"Well, when Ah ketch dis one Ah'm after an' then one more, Ah'll have two," replied John.

How John Caused His Boss-Man To Lose a Hundred Dollars

John's Boss-man, Colonel Clemons, got a lot of pleasure out of betting, and most of the time he won, because we was a shrewd man who did not mind doing wrong. He would even fool his own brother for a dollar. Most of the time, though, he won by trickery and taking advantage of the people he bet with.

One day the Colonel's brother-in-law, who owned a plantation on the other side of the Mississippi River, came over with his family to visit the Colonel. The brother-in-law liked to bet, too. While he and the Colonel were walking around over the plantation, looking at the crops, they kept trying to think of something they could bet on. Colonel Clemons happened to look twards the horse lot and saw John feeding the mules and horses. That gave him an idea.

He had always warned John that he would whip him within an inch of his life if he ever butted in on a conversation while he was talking to another white man. So the Colonel offered to bet one hundred dollars that none of his hands would butt in on white men's conversation.

They walked down to the horse lot where John was feeding the mules. When they got within a few feet of John they stopped and started talking. As soon as John had given the mules their hay, he came over and stood near them and listened, but he did not say a thing. They talked for one whole hour about all sorts of subjects, and still John didn't make a sound. The Colonel's brother-in-law was sure he had lost; so he said, "Well, I reckon I might as well pay you this hundred dollars and go on home and eat that possum with those Irish potatoes all around him."

John touched him on the shoulder quickly and said, "Boss, yuh doesn't cook possums wid Irish taters; yuh cooks 'em wid sweet taters."

And that is how John caused the Colonel to lose one hundred dollars.

JOHN, HIS BOSS-MAN AND THE CATFISH

The Colonel would not allow John and the other hands to fish in the river, but occasionally after the crops were planted and the cotton had been chopped, he would let them fish in the slough on the plantation. And this was only under one condition – that they catch perch only. If a hand caught a catfish he was to throw it back in the water. If the Colonel caught a hand carrying a catfish home, he would take his black-snake whip and give him a good whipping. The Colonel said that catfish were too good for black people.

Most of the hands had stopped fishing, because the perch were so small that they were hardly worth the grease it took to fry them; and then, too, the children were always getting choked on the bones.

John was the only one who kept on fishing down in the

slough. He caught catfish all right, but was clever enough to get them home and have Mariah cook them without getting caught. He would always wait until he saw the Colonel and his family leave for a visit to some neighboring plantation or to the little town down on the river before he went fishing.

One Saturday afternoon when the Colonel left the plantation and started towards town, John told Joseph and David to get his fishing pole from under the cabin. He put it on his shoulder and went down to his regular fishing place. He had been there about two hours when he heard something in the grass behind him. Looking back, he saw the Colonel walking toward the spot where he was fishing. He had caught a seven-pound mud-cat and had tied it on a string to a stab in the ground on the bank of the slough and he was terribly frightened.

Before he could get over his scare the Colonel came up to where he was sitting and said, "John, how is your luck today?" He was looking straight at the catfish.

John pulled up the stob, took the string off, and began working with it.

"Yuh know, boss," said John, "Ah been havin' a awful hard time wid dis catfish; Ah been fishin' fer perch an' dis catfish been stealin' mah bait all day, so Ah, jus' tied 'im up here on de bank to keep 'im off o' mah bait so's Ah could ketch some perches – but A'h *thoo fishin' now*, so Ah mought as well turn 'im loose."

And before Colonel Clemons could answer, the catfish was swimming down the slough. John then went on over to where he had the perch tied, took them out of the water, shouldered his pail, and went on home.

John and His Boss-Man's Best Buggy-Horse

John was a hero not only to the hands of the Clemons Farm, but also to the hands on the other plantations in the neighborhood. He was a hard worker, and he was also the best "'figure-caller" they could find for the Saturday night dances given on the various plantation. No dance was a real success unless John called the figures. All the hands and their women folk liked to hear him sing out, "Swing yo' pardner," and the other commands to the square dance or the cakewalk. John enjoyed calling the figures, too, and he never missed a dance if he could help it.

It happened that one year during the plowing season a special ball was being given on one of the plantations, and visitors from away down on the Gulf of Mexico were expected. One of the mules was sick that day and the Colonel told John to hitch up and plow a beautiful bay horse that the Colonel had just bought. The horse had plenty of spirit and John took a liking to him; so he a:sked the Colonel to let him drive him to the ball. But Colonel Clemons said no.

John was disappointed, because he wanted to show the horse off before all the people at the ball; so he waited until the Colonel and his family were sound asleep, and then slipped out to the horse-lot and caught the horse and hitched him up to the Colonel's new rubber-tired buggy. Then he drove over to the plantation where the dance was being held. He hitched the horse to one of the fence posts and ran over to the dance platform where the crowd was waiting for him to call the figures.

As soon as John climbed upon the platform, the fiddler started playing and John began to call. Everything went fine for an hour. Everybody was laughing and dancing and having a good time when all of a sudden a big 'black fell ow came running toward the platform yelling, "Whose fine horse is dat out dere dead?"

When John heard this, he was badly frightened. He jumped down off the platform, and ran as fast as he could to the post where he had hitched the Colonel's horse. When he got there he found the horse dead. He borrowed a heavy wagon and got some of the hands to help him haul the horse back to the Colonel's plantation. They put the dead horse in the lot and John went back to the ball.

Next morning, John saw a crowd of the other hands on the plantation gathered around the dead horse. He rushed down to the lot, ran up to the Colonel, and said, "Boss, dat hoss Ah plowed yestiddy, is he dead?"

And this time John really put one over on his Boss-man.

How John Stopped His Boss-man From Dreaming

John had just finished eating his Sunday dinner and was seated on the steps of his cabin whittling with his pocket knife on a piece of the lumber left over from the new barn that had been built on Colonel Clemon's plantation that week, when he looked up and saw the Colonel walking across the cotton fields toward his cabin. John knew that the Colonel was on his way to make his regular Sunday afternoon call in order to fuss at him about something or to see what Mariah had cooked for dinner. Colonel Clemons was not satisfied at mistreating the hands all week but he even meddled around the cabins and worried them on Sunday.

While John was wondering what the Colonel was going to fuss about this time, Colonel Clemons walked up, spoke to John and sat down beside him on the steps. "John," he said, "I'll tell you what – let's make a bargain; we both dream a lot, so let's agree that everything I dream you'll see to it that I get it and everything you dream I will see to it that you get it."

"Awright," said John. "Dat suits me."

Next morning before daybreak John was down at the Colonel's house knocking on the door.

"What you want, you fool," yelled the Colonel, "come waking me up this time of morning."

"'Boss," replied John, "you know what Ah dreamed last night? Ah dreamed yuh gimme forty acres an' a mule."

"All right," replied the Colonel, cursing John. "Go and take them, and don't come down here again so early in the morning."

When the next day came, however, the Colonel was down at John's cabin before daybreak. When John heard him knock, he jumped out of bed and ran to the door. The Colonel was standing on the doorsteps.

"John," he said, "I dreamed last night that you gave me that mule and that forty acres back."

"Awright," said John. "Go on an' take 'em."

But the next morning John was down at the Colonel's house again before sunup knocking on his door. The Colonel rushed to the door and said, "Didn't I tell you not to wake me up this early in the morning?"

"Sho, Boss, sho," replied John, "but Ah wanted to tell yuh de dream Ah had before it slipped mah remembrance; Ah dreamed yuh gimme dat mule an' dat forty acres back an' forty acres more."

"All right," said the Colonel, slamming the door in John's face and stamping on the floor, "go on and take them."

The next morning before sunrise, however, John heard somebody rapping on his door again. Before he could open it, he heard the Colonel yelling, "John, John, wake up; you know what I dreamed last night? I dreamed that you gave me back all that I gave you yesterday and that we didn't dream no more."

And this is how John stopped Colonel Clemons from dreaming.

JOHN, MCGRUDER, AND THE BOSS-MAN'S MULE

Of all the hands on the Clemons Plantation, John liked McGruder best. He and John were the only hands on the Clemons Farm that hard been kept by the Colonel when the slaves were freed. For this reason they were the best of friends. Another reason why John was fond of McGruder was that he could always play some prank on him. John had learned to read and write and count since freedom, while McGruder could neither read nor write and could count only to ten. So John had a good deal of fun out of knowing things his friend didn't know.

McGruder was a good marksman, however, and owned

an old double-barrel shotgun that the Colonel had laid aside as unfit for use. John was a poor shot and did not have a gun, but sometimes McGruder invited him to go with him down into the woods to hunt. When they returned home McGruder would always divide whatever, game he had killed with John.

One winter day, when the cotton had all been picked and bacon was scarce at the Colonel's commissary, McGruder decided that he would go down into the woods and kill some rabbits and squirrels for dinner. He asked John to go along with him because he knew that if Colonel Clemons caught him with any game besides possum John would be clever enough to get them out of it.

They had not gone far into the woods before a rabbit jumped up in the weeds and McGruder killed it.

"We killed a rabbit, didn't we?" said John.

"Yeah, we killed a rabbit," replied McGruder.

In a few minutes McGruder sighted some squirrels playing high up among the branches of a tall tree. He took aim with his gun and killed two of them.

"We killed some squirrels, didn't we?" said John.

"Yeah, we killed some squirrels," replied McGruder.

And then, since it was almost twelve o'clock, McGruder decided that he would take the rabbit and the squirrels or home so his wife could cook them for dinner. As they came in sight of the Big House, McGruder saw a bunch of quails flying low and took a shot at them. But instead of the shots striking the birds, they went past them into the Colonel's lot and killed one of his mules.

The Colonel heard the shot and saw the mule fall. He ran to where John and McGruder stood trembling with fear.

"Who killed my mule?" he shouted.

"We did," answered McGruder.

"We, nothin'," replied John. "You killed dat mule yo'self. Ah ain't got no gun."

John, McGruder, and the Bear in the Cornfield

Someone had been taking corn from Colonel Clemson's best cornfield every night for a whole month. He was terribly worried about it; so he made John go down to the field one night to try and catch the thief. John took some old breeches, some quilts, and a feather pillow and made himself a pallet near the edge of the field on the side next to the large stretch of woods, where he might see anybody who came toward the corn field from that direction.

John lay awake watching for a long time but no thief came, and he finally dozed off to sleep. About four o'clock in the morning he was aroused by a noise coming from the direction of the woods, but it was so dark he could not see what it was.

In a few minutes the prowler reached the corn field and started pulling corn.

"A black thievin' rascal," said John, thinking it was one of the hands on the plantation, "out here stealin' the Colonel's corn evuh night - Ah'm gonna ketch 'im dis time."

With these words, John got up from the pallet, walked up behind the rogue, and was about to put his arms around him when he discovered that the prowler was a big black bear. John decided he'd better be leaving, and the bear left right behind him. They reached a tree, but John didn't have time to climb it. They went around and around it until the bear caught up with him and grabbed him by one hand. The bear held on like a vice. John remained on one side of the tree and the bear on the other. When the bear would start around on the side where John was, John would move to the other side. This went on until daybreak, and probably would have kept up all day if McGruder had not happened along hunting rabbits.

McGruder rushed up to the tree and said, "John, what is yuh doin'?"

"Ah'm takin' dis bear home," replied John.

"Why don't yuh lemme kill 'im ?" said McGruder raising

his gun to fire.

"Naw suh," replied John, "Ah wanted to take 'im home alive, but Ah tells you what yuh kin do; yuh come 'ere an' hold 'im while Ah rests awhile."

McGruder laid his gun down on the ground, went over to the tree and caught the bear by one of his paws. The bear let go of John's hand and grabbed McGruder.

John started running towards the plantation, yelling back to McGruder, "Dat wuz mah bear, but he's yo' bear now."

How John Got McGruder's Chickens

Every year when the chickens got to be plentiful on the large plantations, John and McGruder would take some large sacks and make trips two or three nights each week to the chicken houses. They always went together. One of them would watch while the other took the chickens off the roost. In this way they were never caught stealing. They always came back with five or six fat hens or frying-sized chickens.

One night, however, when John went down to McGruder's cabin to look for him, he was not at home. John searched the entire plantation but couldn't find him anywhere. But early the next morning, when John was on his way to the mule lot to feed the mules and horses, who should come towards him with his chicken sack slung across his shoulder but McGruder?

"Where you been?" said John. "Ah been lookin' fer you all night long."

"Ah been out hustlin'," replied McGruder.

"What did you git?" said John.

"Chickens," replied McGruder. "Guess how many Ah's got in dis sack, and Ah'll give you both of 'em."

"Two," said John.

"Humph," said McGruder," somebody musta tol' you."

And this is how John got McGruder's chickens.

Why John Went Hungry One Day

Colonel Clemons had a hard time thinking of enough tasks for all of the hands on the plantation to do in the winter time. It was an easy matter to find jobs during the harvest and the growing seasons. The planting season kept them busy, too, but in the winter there wasn't much work to do in the fields.

Colonel Clemons just hated to see the hands resting; so he bought a one-hundred-acre cypress grove about six miles from his plantation. After this, when winter came and there was nothing to do in the fields, he would send the hands down to the grove to cut down the trees and make them into ties to sell to the railroad companies.

One Sunday, John's wife, Mariah, had cooked a big Sunday dinner – chicken, cake, and pie. So she saved some of it and fixed John a nice lunch Monday morning to take with him down to the cypress grove.

John was a little late starting to work that morning; so he walked fast and ran part of the way because he was afraid the Colonel would see him. On the way he dropped his lunch. He didn't miss it until he got where, the other hands were at work, when he felt in his pocket and realized it was gone. He turned right around and started back up the lane to look for it.

He had gone about half a mile when he met McGruder, who had also started to work late that morning. McGruder was wiping his mouth with his hand.

John walked up to him and said, "Did yuh find a lunch down there in de lane?"

"Naw," replied McGruder. "Couldn't a dog found it an' et it up well as Ah could?"

So John had to go hungry all that day.

How John Caused McGruder To Starve Almost to Death

One year they had a drought in the section where Colonel Clemons lived. The Colonel felt that his crops were all going to fail; so he was meaner than ever. He cussed and fussed at John and the other hands all of the time. Besides, he gave them only one-half as much groceries as he had given them before and that was scarcely enough to keep them from starving to death.

Everybody was working harder, yet they could never please the Colonel; so one evening John went down to McGruder's cabin looking very sad. McGruder noticed how unhappy John was and asked him what was the matter with him.

"Nothin'" replied John. "Ah just cussed de Colonel out good today, dat's all."

"Yuh did?," said McGruder.

"Yeah," answered John, "Ah cussed him out good."

The next day McGruder decided that when the Colonel came up to him in the field and started complaining about the amount of work he was doing, he was going to cuss him out, too, just like John.

About an hour before quitting time that evening McGruder saw the Colonel walking towards him looking very angry. He knew that trouble was on the way, and when the Colonel came up and started fussing at him for being slow, McGruder started cussing him out. The Colonel knocked him down and made him stay in the field and work until ten o'clock that night. Then he went to McGruder's cabin and took all of his groceries away from him, and told him that he was not going to get anything else to eat for a week.

That night about eleven o'clock when John went over to McGruder's cabin, McGruder said, "John, how come you could cuss de Colonel out an' he didn' hit you an' take all o' yo groceries lack he done mine?"

"Hump," said John. "Yuh didn't ast me if he heard me."

And that is the way John got even with McGruder for eating his lunch he lost on the way to the cypress grove during the winter.

JOHN, MCGRUDER, AND THE BARREL OF APPLES

Once each month Colonel Clemens took John and McGruder and went down to his commissary on the river to get the month's supply of groceries for himself and his hands and feed for the stock. John drove the grocery wagon and McGruder drove the feed wagon.

One year on the second Saturday in December, when John and McGruder went with the Colonel down to the commissary to get the supplies for Christmas, they saw a large shipment of apples being unloaded from a freight train. Because they were so busy, the clerks didn't have time to carry the barrels inside as they were unloaded from the freight cars, but left them out behind the store.

While John and McGruder were carrying the groceries and the feed to the wagons, they started thinking how nice it would be to take one of the barrels of apples home with them. They could bury it in the ground until Christmas and then dig it up and fill the children's stockings with apples on Christmas Eve night.

So that night they stole a barrel of apples. Since it was moonlight, they decided to divide the apples that same night, so John started counting them out. "One for you, and one for me," he said, placing one apple on the right hand side of the barrel for himself, and one on the left hand side of the barrel for McGruder.

"Two for you," continued John, putting one apple in McGruder's pile, "and two for me," he said, dropping two apples in his pile. "Three for you," he went on while throwing one more apple in McGruder's pile, "and one, two three for me," this time letting three apples fall in his pile.

John continued in this manner, never giving McGruder more than one apple at a time, but always, giving himself the exact number mentioned. When he had taken all of the apples out of the barrel, McGruder, who could not count, but who had been watching his pile and John's pile and comparing the size of them, said, "John, is yuh countin' dem apples right?"

"Sho Ah is, fool," said John. Didn' yuh hear me countin' 'em; evuh time Ah took one Ah give you one; when Ah took two Ah give you two."

"Well, is dey as many apples in yo' pile as dey is in mine?"

"Sho dey is," replied John.

"Well den," said McGruder, "Ah'll jes take yo' pile."

How McGruder's Prayer Was Answered

McGruder was the last hand on the plantation to join the church. He and his wife Susan were both kind of simpleminded and did not understand religion. The preacher was always disgusted when he went down to McGruder's cabin to try persuading Susan to join the church.

One Saturday when the preacher went down to talk to her about religion, he said, "Sister Susan, how about comin' an' goin' to Heaben wid me?"

"Well, Ah don't know," replied Susan. "McGruder been talkin' 'bout goin' up to Arkansaw dis week; if'n he don't go up there Ah might go wid yuh."

"Sister," continued the preacher, "you kinda livin' in de dark, ain't yuh?"

"Yeah," replied Susan, "Ah been tellin' McGruder to git de Colonel to put some windows in de cabin but he ain't never did hit."

This disgusted the preacher so much that he never did go back to talk with Susan anymore, but John kept on talking to McGruder until he persuaded him to join the church. John told him if he joined the church, the Lord would give him anything he prayed for, and more than anything else McGruder wanted a milch-cow like John's.

John had told McGruder that the way to pray and get what you wanted was to pick out a tree in the woods, go to it every night, get down on your knees beneath it, and ask the Lord for what you wanted. So McGruder went down into the woods near the plantation on the Monday night after he joined the church, picked himself out a big tree, got down on his knees beneath it, and started playing.

"Oh Lawd," he said, "please sen' me ten dollars to buy me a cow like John's cow. Oh, Lawd, please sen' me ten dollars to buy me a cow like John's cow."

John did not see McGruder go down into the woods, but John's little boys, Joseph and David, saw him and told their father about seeing McGruder go down to the pasture Monday night to pray. The next night John took the little boys with him and asked them to show him the tree that McGruder had prayed under. The little boys pointed a big liveoak tree out to him. John climbed the tree and had hardly hidden himself when McGruder made his appearance. He got down on his knees and started praying. "Oh, Lawd," he said, "please sen' me ten dollars to buy me a cow like John's cow."

When John heard McGruder's prayer he dropped a five-dollar bill down from the tree and said, "McGruder, here's a five-dollar bill; come back tomorrow night and Ah'll give you some more to help you buy a cow like John's cow."

McGruder thought that John was the Lord. He picked up the five-dollar bill, put it in his pocket and said, "Awright, Lawd, Ah'll be heah."

The next night John got to the tree first again and hid in its branches. In a little while McGruder came. He got down on his knees and started praying.

"Oh Lawd," he said, "please sen' me five dollors mo' to buy me a cow like John's cow."

John dropped a one-dollar bill down to him from the top of the tree and said, "McGruder, here's another dollar to help you buy a cow like John's cow. Now Ah tell you what do; take the five-dollar bill that Ah give you las' night and the one dollar that I give you tonight and leave 'em both under the tree and go on home, and tomorrow night when you come back, Ah'll give you a ten-dollar bill."

"Naw suh, Lawd, dat's awright," replied McGruder, getting up off his knees, "'Ah sho thanks you fer de six, 'but

Ah'll get de other fo' some place else."

And this is how McGruder's prayer was answered.

JOHN AND THE DICE GAME

Cotton picking season was the time of year that the hands on the Southern plantation had most money, but this was only true when they had a good crop year. Whenever these good crop years came, John and several of the hands on the other plantations always gambled. They usually went down to Colonel Clemon's cotton gin every Sunday afternoon and shot dice until the sun went down and it got too dark to see. There were always a large number of bales of cotton there on Sunday, so the crapshooters hid behind the bales of cotton where they could not be seen.

None of the white folks knew that gambling was going on at the gin until Steve, one of the hands from another plantation, lost a lot of money on Sunday and accused some of the others of cheating in the game. It happened that Steven went to town the next Saturday. While there, he visited the sheriff's office and told him about John and the other hands gambling every Sunday afternoon, down at the Colonel's gin. So the sheriff took two deputies with him out to the Colonel's plantation the next Sunday and arrested the gamblers.

When the day for the trial came, the Judge questioned each one of the hands separately as to his guilt or innocence. John was the last one called to the stand. The others had been tried, found guilty, and fined ten dollars for gambling. Everybody in the court-room was wondering whether or not John, who could usually get himself out of trouble, was going to be able to fool the Judge this time and keep from paying a fine.

When John's turn came, the Judge called him to the stand. Everybody was so quiet you could hear a pin drop in the courtroom.

"John," said the Judge, "didn't I tell you the last time you were here that I would fine you if I ever caught you winning money in games of chance?"

"Yas suh, Judge," replied John, "but Ah wasn't winning. Ah was losin'."

And this is how John got out of paying a fine for shooting dice.

JOHN'S LITTLE BOYS AND THE NEW PREACHER

John and Mariah were the most faithful members of the little Baptist church down on the river. The preacher came once each month – every fourth Sunday – to preach to the hands on the Colonel's plantation, and the members had an agreement that he would always stay at John's cabin. He slept there and ate his meals there also.

John's wife, Mariah, was always tickled to have the honor of having the preacher stop with her on Saturday and Sunday. When he was there, Mariah cooked two or three chickens for dinner each day; so John's little boys, Joseph and David were also glad when the preacher came, because they knew they were going to have chicken for dinner.

One fourth Sunday the regular preacher took sick and could not travel; so he sent a new preacher to preach in his place. Mariah treated him just as she treated the old preacher. She put a big dish of chicken on the table for him that Saturday just as she had always done when the old preacher came. She then sent the little boys out in the yard to play, while she, John, and the preacher ate. When Mariah called Joseph and David to dinner, the first thing the two boys did was to look at the chicken platter and see that it was empty.

"Where's de chicken?" they asked. The preacher, who had eaten up all the chicken and was still seated at the table pointed to the gravy bowl and said, "Eat jayvee; jayvee's good."

After church services Sunday morning Mariah filled up the big dish with chicken again and placed it on the table. On the table was a long red oil cloth so long that a person could hide underneath it without being seen. So while Mariah was looking at a hoe cake she had cooking in a skillet in the fireplace, Joseph and David took the chicken off the table, got under the table with it, and ate it all up.

When the bread was done Mariah called John and the new preacher in to dinner. They came in, sat down at the table, said the blessing and got ready to eat. Then the preacher looked for the chicken platter, but it was nowhere to be seen. He said, "Where's de chicken?"

Joseph, the oldest boy, stuck his head out from under the table and yelled, "Eat jayvee; jayvee's good."

JOHN AND THE TWO WHITE MEN IN COURT

One year the boll-weevils got into the cotton crop on Colonel Clemons' plantation and destroyed most of it. This made times very hard for the Colonel, and since he did not make any money, he did not provide sufficient food and clothing for the hands. So naturally they stole anything they could get away with.

Never a week passed that some of the hands were not arrested and carried to jail.

One day the sheriff came out to Colonel Clemons' farm and arrested John. With him were two white hands he had arrested on a neighboring plantation. John and the two white hands were all charged with stealing and they were to be tried on the same day at the same hour.

When John and the two white men were brought in to the court room and arraigned for trial, John was very nervous and was trembling. This was the first time in his life that he had not been able to think of an excuse. He knew, however that they were going to try the white men first; so he decided to listen to their answers and imitate them when his turn came.

The first case called was that of one of the white hand who was accused of stealing a horse.

"Guilty, or not ,guilty," said the judge.

"Not guilty," replied the man; "I've owned that horse ever since he was a colt." The case was dismissed.

Then the Judge called the second white man to the stand. He was accused of stealing a cow. "Guilty, or not guilty asked the Judge.

"Not guilty," replied the defendant; "I've owned that cow ever since she was a calf." The case was dismissed.

Then John was called to the stand. He was accused of stealing a wagon.

"Guilty, or not guilty," demanded the Judge.

"Not Guilty," replied John. "Ah' s owned dat wagon ever since it was a wheelbarrow."

JOHN AND THE DOCTOR

The nearest town to Colonel Clemons' plantation was twenty-five miles away. John would have liked to go to town every Saturday afternoon, but the Colonel would not take him unless there were groceries, lumber, or farm tools to be loaded, on the wagon. Some of the other plantation owners, however would take John to town anytime he wanted to go. They did this without expecting him to do any work for them, too. The only requirement was that John be at the hitching post at the courthouse square at six o'clock, the time they always started back to their plantations.

John was usually there waiting at six o'clock, but one Saturday, in the month of February, he didn't show up. He had carried his little boys, Joseph and David, with him to see his sister, who cooked for the banker. He left the little boys with his sister and went down to the saloon.

While he was in the saloon a blizzard came up and the bartender made a hot fire in the air-tight heater. This made John very drowsy and he went to sleep. It was ten 'o'clock at night when John's sister and the little boys found him asleep in the saloon. The other hands and all of the plantation owners had gone home. It had rained, too, and the ground had frozen over. It was the coldest day the South had had for thirty years; so it was impossible for John and the children to walk home. They would have frozen to death. When his sister woke him up, John went down to the livery stable and asked the owner how much he would charge him to rent a horse and buggy. The man told him it would cost him ten dollars. John did not have ten dollars; so he could not get the horse and buggy. He was scratching his head and wondering how he was going to get his little boys home, when he looked across the street and saw the doctor's sign. He also noticed that the doctor's horse and buggy were in front of the house; so he walked across the street, stepped up on the doctor's porch and knocked on the door.

The doctor opened the door and invited him in. "Doc," said John, "kin you make a call out tuh mah house right away?"

"Certainly," replied the doctor.

"Awright suh," said John. "Let's go."

So John and the little boys got in the buggy with the doctor and pulled the laprobe around them tight to keep their legs warm, and the doctor drove them out to the Colonel's plantation.

When they reached John's cabin, John pulled out a five-dollar bill, handed it to the doctor, and started in the house.

"Wait a minute," said the doctor. "Who's sick?"

"Nobody,' replied John. "Ah didn' have money nuff to hire a horse and buggy to bring me home, an' Ah knowed yo' calls wuz cheaper'n de livery-stable."

And this is how John, Joseph, and David got home that cold winter's night.

JOHN AND THE CONSTABLE

There were not only a large number of rabbits, possums, and squirrels in the stretches of woods on the Southern plantations but also deer.

There was no law against killing the other wild animals but at a certain season of the year it was against the law to kill a deer. If anyone killed a deer at this time, he was arrested and taken to jail; then he was tried and fined twenty five dollars.

Most of the plantations had woods filled with deer, but Colonel Clemons had cut down most of the trees on his plantation and planted cotton, sugar cane, and corn on the land. Directly across the road from the Colonel's plantation however, was a large forest owned by the Colonel's brother so John went with McGruder every year during this season of the year to the Colonel's brother's farm to hunt and kill deer.

McGruder would kill the deer and John would sell them. Then they would divide the money. John knew exactly how to sell them. He was well acquainted with all the sheriffs and constables in that part of the country. He also knew the men who came out to the plantation every year to buy the deer that McGruder killed. Consequently he and McGruder had never been caught. They had regular customers.

This went on for four years. One Saturday John, McGruder, and John's little boys went to hunt deer. Just as John and McGruder were about to get through the barbed-wire fence and go into the Colonel brother's thickly wooded forest the little boys looked up and saw a white man driving a pot-bellied horse to an old wobbly buggy coming towards them. John's first impulse was to move on, but as they had not been able to sell many deer that year, he decided to wait and see whether the man might be one of their customers.

But as the man came nearer they realized that he was stranger, so John decided to let him pass without speaking to him. But the man stopped, got out of his buggy and walked over to where John, McGruder, and the little boys were standing.

Singling John out, he asked, "Do you know where I can buy a deer?"

John hesitated at first, but finally he said, "Sho, boss, sho. Ah don' have none now but Ah kin git you one in 'bout a houah."

John was all smiles; he saw five dollars apiece in sight now for him and McGruder – their luck was coming back.

"How do you know you can?" asked the stranger, while

John was grinning over the almost certain sale of the deer.

"Cause," replied John, "me an' mah pardner jes' kilt one yistiddy down in dat stretch o' woods 'cross de road."

"You did?" said the stranger, "And do you know who I am?"

"Naw suh, naw sub," replied John. "Who is yuh?"

"Well," answered the stranger pulling back his coat and showing a badge, "I'm the biggest constable in the South."

"Says yuh is, Bos, says yuh is," replied John. "Well, know who Ah is? Ah's de biggest liar in de South."

--SEVEN--
MORE TRUTH THAN POETRY

This volume of poetry, published in 1947, shows J. Mason Brewer at his sardonic best. The volume also includes marvelous drawings by H. E. Johnson; however we are not able to reprint them. Brewer inscribed the book for the readers: "May the lines penned in this volume bring added joy and inspiration to you, and contribute substantially to your knowledge and understanding of the American Negro and his problems." He divided the work into four parts, the first "People of the Soul," the second, "Patriotic and Eulogistic verse," the third "Verse of Protest," and fourth, "Downright City Folks." It probably comes as no surprise that Brewer provides us with understanding as well as "more truth than poetry."

Originally published as J. Mason Brewer, *More Truth Than Poetry* (Austin, Texas: privately printed, 1947). Reprinted by permission.

PART I
PEOPLE OF THE SOUL

Reverend Johnson's Convention Prayer

Ah thanks you Lawd fer wakin' me up, dis mawnin' at half pass fo'
'Cause you knowed dat mah ole Chevrolay travels kind a slow,
An'ah thanks you dat Miz Johnson had mah breakfas' on de plate,
An' mah coffee in de coffee pot, n'ah didn't haft uh wait.
Ah thanks you Lawd, when ah went out ter look at mah ole car,
Dat dey wuzn't narry puncture in de fo' wheels stan'nin' dar,
Ah thanks you dat hit started, when ah shove de starter in,
An' ah didn't haft uh pester, wid dat thing uh-mah-doo ergin.
Ah thanks yuh dat mah smokin' pipe, wuz layin' in de seat,
Ob de car·an' dat Miz Johnson, wrapped me up a bite to eat.
Ah thanks yuh dat ah seed hit, fo' ah lef de Kitchen step,
Ah dat my smokin' 'baccuh wuz in de pocket whar hit's kep.

Ah thanks you dat dat car Ah met--whar de 'oman could jes half see;
Ah thanks you Lawd fer keepin' hit fum runnin' in tuh me;
An' ah thanks you Lawd; Ah thanks yuh, dat you didn't lemme pass
Dat Good-Gulf fillin' station when ah's mos' run out o' gas.
Ah thanks you dat ah had mah jack, when mah lef hin' tire blowed out
An'ah thanks you Lawd—dat ah ain't weak—dat ah's still kinda stout;
Ah thanks yuh Lawd fer givin' me, de strenth to' change dat tiah;

An when mah front car do' comed loose--ah had dat bailin'
wire.

Ah thanks yuh Lawd fer showin' me, dat ole soul sides duh
road
A hobblin 'long erpon dat stick, an carryin' dat heaby load;
Ah thanks yuh dat ah have de time, to stop an' let her ride;
An' ah thanks yuh Lawd fer easin', de misery in her side,
Ah thanks yuh Lawd fer gittin' me to de meetin' on de
houah,
An dat mah frock-tail coat staid dry, when we runned into
dat showah;
An' now Dear Lawd, ah Thanks yuh, whilst ahs down heah
on mah knees
Fer sendin' thoo de window--dat sweet an' coolin' breeze.

Ah thanks yuh Lawd, dat ah kin raise, mah poly voice, ergin
In de Mount Moriah Convention, Ah thanks yuh Sah,
A-Men!

Dat's Uh Norther

Heah dat win' uh whistlin'?
See dem tree limbs shake?
Heah dem leaves uh rustlin'?
Heah duh noise dey make?
See dem geeses flyin'
To'a'ds duh gulf ergin?
See dem dark clouds sailin'?
Listen at dat win!
Dat's uh Norther!

Martha, close duh winduh!
Jim, put on dat shoe!
Lias, stir dat fiah up!
What am wrong wid you?
Don't you heah duh rattlin'
Of dat winduh pane?
Don't you heah duh patter
Of dat sleet an' rain?
Dat's uh Norther!

Go an git dat kivver
Unnuhneaf duh bed,
Is you thoo wid suppuh?
Am duh mules all fed?
Bring dat ole sack tuh me!
Lemme stop dis crack;
Feels uh pain uh nunnin'
Up an' down mah back.
Dat's uh Norther!

Colored Day At The Orangeburg Fair

There's nothing more interesting, anywhere
Than Colored Day at the Orangeburg Fair,
Where colored folk from the farms aroun'
Mingling with those who reside in town
Form a heterogeneous throng
Milling about the whole day long.

Country Belles from Bowman-Utah;
Little Bitty Children with Ma and Pa;
Young Jitterbugs--age sixteen
All form a part of the Colored Day Scene,
As well as infants--milk bottle in hand
Who holler and cry as loud as they can.

All day long, the dark folk go
Up and down, from show to show;
First in this place--then in that;
Scarcely knowing where they are at;
Only knowing that it's the Fair
And they're glad that they are there.

All throughout the livelong day
They stroll around the whole Mid-way
Eating hamburger, or hot-dog bun
And having themselves a lot of fun;
Going in this way, and coming out that;
Looking at midgets, and people, too fat.

Gazing at snake, or crocodile
Then after resting a little while
They crowd into the Harlem Show,
And fill up every single row
To hear the Colored Fair Swing Band,
And a brown girl sing "Aint Got No Man."

Then again, they come outside
And take some kind," or other ride
Upon the many things they see
Depending on the price, or fee;
Hobby-horse, or Ferris Wheel
Whichever has the most appeal.
Then finally when it's time to go
The Country Folks put on a show
By going to the Broadcast Stand,
And calling for some girl or man
In accents loud they blaze away,
And this is what you hear them say.

"Abe Jones' girl-frien', who is louse
Meet him up at duh Zippity House."
He doesn't mean the girl's a chinch,
Nor is he trying to talk in French;
He means he'd like to see her face
Up at the Fair Exhibit place.

Then, when at last they all are found
They get together and leave the grounds;
Some in trucks and automobiles,
Or anything else that rolls on wheels;
They leave, but their money, this year's crop share
Still remains at the County Fair.

Jes Piddlin'

Ah aint workin', naw suh!
Ah aint doin' much o' nothin'
Ah'm jes killin' time puttin' uh picket o' two in dis ol' fence whar deys needed mos';
'Fo ah gits thoo mought straighten up dat ol' one sided pos'
Jes piddlin'.

Mos' duh days ah grabs uh hammer an' nails, an dis ol' hoe--
Ah'm jes messin' 'roun' choppin' uh weed o' so out o' de garden whar dey chokes de peas;
'Fo dark liable tuh sharpen mah ax
An' whack down one o' dese trees
Jes piddlin'.

Sometimes takes de mules down tuh de tank tuh gib 'em uh drink--
An' brings 'em back tuh de house 'fo dey hitches 'em up an' takes 'em tuh de fiel'
'Min's me while ah's got dis monkey wrench better tighten up dis hin' wagon wheel
Jes piddlin'.

PART II
PATRIOTIC AND EULOGISTIC VERSE

Cullud Hist'ry Week

[Dedicated to Principal L. Virgil Williams of the Booker T. Washington High School of Dallas, Texas, February 14, 1934, because of his initiative and sincere interest in promoting the observance of NATIONAL NEGRO HISTORY WEEK in Dallas, Texas.]

Wuz you down tuh duh Chu'ch House Sunday
When duh Pre'chuh take his tex'?
Dat wuz one time dat he preached hit
Widout takin' off his specks.
Well, he take his tex' in Romans--
He say "Less be proud, not meek;
Ah wants all yuh folks tuh know 'bout
Dis am Cullud Hist'ry Week."

Den he go on talkin' 'bout hit
'Bout duh great men we done had—
Dis duh fus time ah done been dere
Dat he didn't make me mad.
Seem lack he' wuz full o' powuh
 Ez he hist his han' an' speak
Tellin' all erbout duh prog'am
Of duh Cullud Hist'ry Week.
Well suh, dat dere got me staa'ted
Out tuh etchin' fer some mo',
So ah look down at duh prog'am
 So's tuh fine out whar tuh go
Fer tuh heah some mo' dese speeches
An' some mo' speechmakers speak

So's tuh fine out 'bout mah people
Durin' Cullud Hist'ry Week.

So ah gits tuh all duh meetin's
Fum duh fus 'un tuh duh las';
Kinda felt lack ah wuz studyin'
Lack yuh does in Night School Class,
An' ah tuck in so much learnin'
Dat ah foun' out whar tuh seek
Fer 'duh bes' dat life kin gib us
Durin' Cullud Hist'ry Week.

Now duh High School staa't duh thing off,
Case dey hab uh course up dere
Dat dey teaches High Up students
'Bout duh black man evuhwhere;
Ef he wuz uh some 'count pusson
An' He rech duh topmos' peak
Den dey pints him ez uh model
Durin' Cullud Hist'ry Week.

Whar duh white folks has uh Lincoln
We has got uh Booker T.
Whar dey's got uh Franklin Roosevelt
We has got Oscar Depree,
Ah done foun' out all dis bizness
When ah heered speechmakers speak
On duh diffunt kin' o' prog'ams
Durin' Cullud Hist'ry Week.

Negro Heroes In American Wars The Civil War
–Sergeant William H. Carney

After our land was free, the question arose
Should we hold black folks slaves, or free the negroes?
The North thought it best, if the Southern folks would,
But the Southerners did not believe that they should.

The South told the North that it would secede
Before it'd allow its slaves to be freed;
So the question got heated and things went so far
Until our country itself had a war.

The Civil War's what it was called by name,
And the North and the South were both to blame;
For since they had fought and made themselves free
There was certainly no reason they should not agree.

But anyhow after the war began
They took every ablebodied man
And sent him to fight for the side he chose;
For, or against, the enslaved Negroes.

In the North where some of the Negroes were free;
They organized sometimes, a Company
Composed of Negro soldiers alone;
And sometimes, excellent bravery was shown.

A Negro flag bearer, one time was shot down
And the flag of the North almost fell to the ground;
But a sergeant named Carney in Company C
Said, "I'll get our old flag, if the bullets get me."

This occurred at Fort Wagner--he was shot in the thigh;
But he planted the flag on the parapet-high
And he kept it there through the second round

And said, "Boys the old flag never touched the ground."
Sergeant William H. Carney, these noble words said;
With a shot in the thigh, and one in the head;
Though suffering with pain, from more than one wound;
He kept the old flag from touching the ground.

An Ode To George Washington Carver
April 4, 1943

–Written for the Dallas Branch of the N.A.A.C.P. on the Occasion of the Memorial Services Conducted for Dr. Carver, a year after his passing.

He was the soil's reflector,
And he was the seer of its ways;
He was the master detector
Of the earth's sandy loam, and its clays.
He took the yam and the peanut—
The common weeds that grew;
And helped the man who lived in a hut
To build him a home--brand new.

He was the Good Earth's saviour,
Because of his helpful deeds
In studying its plants behaviour,
And making them fill new needs.
He was both prophet and preacher
Of the values inherent in land;
He was research-scientist and teacher
Of plant usages God had planned.

He was also a learned physician,
For often he cured sick trees
That were found in diseased condition
Of all of their maladies.
He would take no remuneration
For the works of his fertile brain;
He was God's gift sent to a nation
To toil without worldly gain.

He was humble in all of his living,
And Christ-like in all of his ways
Never once taking credit, but giving

His creator all of the praise.
He bridged the wide gap between Races—
Transcended the Deep South's moulds;
He is honored in thousands of places
And loved by millions of souls.

Uncle John Pops Off (Dis Am Deh Wah O' De Bible)

Sich another carryin' on ah never seed
Folks just goin' 'long -payin' no heed
Lack de country aint steeped in wah;
De worse un ah have ever saw.
Ah aint never seed in mah days befo'
So many people dat have to go,
Yet it seem lack wid all whats done
Some folks acts lack it's mostly fun.
Womens' still dressin' up, lookin' dey bes'
Mens' buyin' liquor an' drinkin' dat mess
Eatin' dey porkchops an' nibblin' on ham
Forgettin' de worl' am in a turbul jam.
Dey better pay heed cause de Bible done say
Dat de end o' de worl' was comin' dis way.
       Dis am de wah o' de Bible!

De Bible am true--it aint no liar
Didn't it say de Worl'd be 'stroyed by fiah?
An' 'cardin' to what de papers say
Aint dat what dey's doin' in de wah today?
Ah see's in de papers my gran' son buy
Lots o' pitchers wid fiah an' smoke in de sky;
Ah see's lots o' houses and boats in flame
An' dey says dat a fellow name Hitler's to blame.
Dis mought be true, but ah b'lieves it's sin
An' de end o' de worl' is comin' ergin;
It said dat mother'd turn agin son
An' son agin father--aint dis bein' done?
From de North to de South—f'om de Wes' to de Eas'
Dey aint nowhars whar deys quiet an' peace.
       Dis am de wah o' de Bible!

You kin think what you wants to an' 'low what you mus',
  But ah's 'bliged to put de words o' de Bible fus,
  So you better quit rollin' in filth an' mire
  Unker Sam done tuck you often rubber tire,
  An' if ah reads right an' ah unnerstan'
  De jig am up--it's in God's plan.
  De Good Book said dey'd be a beas'
  Dat he'd 'vour de high as well as de leas',
  So it seem lack to me dis Hitler man
  Am fittin' right in to de Judgment plan;
  But it seem also lack he's out on de limb
  An putty soon now'l see de end o' him,
  Cause deys sho gonna be some hell to pay
  If he ever meet up wid de U. S. A.
      Dis am de wah o' de Bible!

PART III
VERSE OF PROTEST

A Negro Veteran of World War II Observes a Governor's Inaugural Day Celebration

Canto I

A great event took place in my home town today;
People swarmed into the city from miles, and miles away
To witness the inauguration of the new Governor of the
    state
Into whose hands had been entrusted its welfare and its
    fate.
You'd have thought the weighty office of deciding what
    was best
Would have made him feel his duties involved more than
    Prejudice, and jest.
But true to traditions he had deep down inside
He said that the state its own policies and proceedings
    would decide;
That there'd be no waiting on the nation, or on Washington,
    D.C.
To say to say what action they should take—that this here state
    was free
To act on certain laws—I suppose he meant like Negroes
    not enrolling
In the State University--to his white listeners this was
    very, very consoling,
But to me, who had fought and bled for America and
    Almost died on a Foreign battle field,
And who now being unable to walk and having to be placed
    in a wheel chair and wheeled
His words were like daggers tearing into my very soul,
And I felt that there was no such thing for me and
    my black brothers as "Let The Good Times Roll."

Canto II

That night they made merry in the lobby of the State Capitol, and at the State University, they sang and danced,
And those who were present seemed happy, and pleasingly entranced.
No black faces were to be seen among the guests and I remembered that my grand-father had seriously objected to having been denied the privilege of attending a similar affair when he served as State Senator, immediately after the Civil War;
Practices hadn't changed much in eighty years; only my father was a porter at the Capitol Building now and they had given him the so-called high privilege of arranging the chairs for the celebration, and washing the Governor's car.
It seemed strange on such a serious occasion that folks could be having such hilarious fun,
But I understood it better when I looked up at a sign across the street from the Capital City's leading theatre (For Whites Only) announcing the World Premiere showing of "It's A Joke Son."

Labor Battalion A La World War I

Dis aint khaki, dis stuff blue;
Got hit on duh whole blame crew;
Wondah's what dey 'tends tuh do?

Lookee yonduh spades an' picks;
Dem two things an' me don't mix;
Wish ah's back home in duh sticks.

Said dey wanted me tuh fight;
An' now case ah cant read an' write
Tries tuh claim dat ah aint bright.

Thought dat when ah got to France
Ah's gonna have uh fightin' chance;
But all ah does is work an' dance.

Too Far Trip

One time I took a trip down
To San Antonio;
I took my boy along with me
To see the Alamo.

We viewed the sacred building,
And then we went to see
The Zoo out at the park there;
He clapped his hands with glee.

We saw some shetland ponies
And he said "Dad let me ride,"
I handed him a nickel;
His dark eyes glowed with pride.

He walked up to the keeper .
And said "I'm riding too."
The keeper gave his money back
And said "This aint for you."

He looked up at the keeper,
And hung his proud head down
And took a pocket mirror out
And saw that he was brown.

Talkin' Bout N.R.A.

Humph! Talkin' 'bout N.R.A.
What Frank Roosevelt say,
Take ten niggers off shif'
Tuh give ten whites uh lif';
Yet dey say hit pay—
Dis heah N.R.A.
Humph! Talkin' 'bout N.R.A.

Talkin' 'bout N.R.A.
Gonna make you gray,
Hours cut tuh six;
Dey's jes up tuh tricks;
Dollars half in two;
What's duh matter'd you?
Humph! Talkin' 'bout N.R.A

Talkin' 'bout N.R.A.
Whar'd you git dat way?
Ah'm uh tellin' yuh Bob;
You aint gittin' no job;
Unless you change yo' skin
You jest aint counted in.
Humph! Talkin' 'bout N.R.A.

Talkin' 'bout N.R.A.
Wastin' words I say;
Eagle, black, o' blue
Aint gwine fly to you,
You jest wastin' breaf
Nigguh haftuh help hisse'f.
Humph! Talkin' 'bout N.R.A.

PART IV
DOWNRIGHT CITY FOLKS

Church Gal

Gonna put on mah Sunday-go-to-meetin's;
Gonna go down tuh Bob's café;
Gonna set down and dring me uh bottle o' pop
So's all duh gals kin say
"Haint dat outfit she got on
Up tuh duh ver' las' minnit?
"Sides dat honey, hit sho fit;
Don't she look good in it?"
Gonna put on mah Sunday-go-tuh-meetings;
Gonna walk pass duh Town Hotel
So's all duh waiters an' cooks kin say
"Don't dat gal look swell?"
Gonna git out mah sto' bought jewl'ry;
Put hit on mah neck an'wris',
An' duh fus'n ghot to cou'age tuh ast me
Ah gwine gib 'im uh kiss.
Gonna put on mah Sunday-go-tuh-meetin's;
Gonna walk down duh Main Church aisle
So's all duh folks in duh pews kin say
"Wonduh who's dat chile?"
Gonna walk up tuh duh colleckshun plate
An' drap uh quarter in,
Ab' wink mah eye at duh preachuh man;
Humph! Dat aint no sin.

Liza Attends Green Pastures

Dis duh bigges' crowd o' people ah's done evuh seed befo'
Look uh dere how dey's uh pushin' an' uh shovin' in duh do'.
 Put yo' elbow out dere honey—rush on in dere wid duh crowd;
 Onlies' thing ah hates erbout hit devlish nigguhs talks so loud.
Git on in duh elevatuh—other folks is fat ez you;
 You acks lack uh ignoramus—lack yuh don't know what to do.
Hand duh tickets dere t'dat nigguh wid duh black frock tail coat on;
 He's duh funnies' lookin' sumpin ah done see'd since ah been bawn.
Dere's duh numbuhs on duh tickets—can't yuh read dere what his say;
Hurry up and seat us nigguh, so dat we kin see duh play;
You don't need tuh make nobody git up fum duh seat dey got;
Keep on foolin' 'roun' heah wid me, you gona up an' make me hot.
Hello dere, gal, whyd'n yuh tell me dat youse comin' tuh duh show?
Jes decided duh las' minit dat you'd kinda lack tuh go.
 Lady, please mam take yo' hat off; how in duh worl' yuh speck me tuh see?
Who's dat skinny li'l' ole woman lookin' crost-eyed dere at me?

Hol' yo watch heah jes uh minnit; ah declare hit's almos' nine;
 Fer ez gittin places promp' lack, nigguh mought ez well quit tryin'.
Bet dey's mo'n two o' three hunnerd down dere now out tuh duh front
Looks tuh me lack ah done waited fer duh curtain mo'n uh mont'.
Here's uh bunch o' high tone people makin' Hist'ry fer duh race

An' uh bunch o' triflin' nigguhs bein' late, dat's uh disgrace.
Lookee dere duh curtain's risin'—looks jes lack uh Sunday
                School;
See duh Preachuh wid his Bible tryin' tuh teach duh
                Golden Rule.

Now duh Lawd an' all his angels up in Heabun kin be seen;
Wonder which one o' dem angels is duh one whut is duh
                Queen?
Well suh, lookee, dere's uh garden, an' uh man an' woman,
                too;
Lookee dere, dey's bof excited; wonder what dey's gonna do.

Oh! mah Lawd, duh man done grab her in his ahms, an'
                she done yell;
Dat dere paa't dere aint so sporty--why duh woman lack tuh fell.
Dem dere mus' be Cain an' Abel--wonder why dey's in uh
                fight?
Don't dey know dat bein' brothers, actin' dat way, jes aint
                right.
Now duh Lawd is talkin' tuh Noah 'bout duh judgment an'
                duh Ark;
You know sum pin dat dere paa't dere got duh platform
                kinda dark.

What's duh matter? Ah been cryin'; dat' s duh why ah shut
                mah mouf;
Dis heah play's erbout duh bes' un dat done evuh come tuh
                duh Souf.

Noah, Pharoah, an' Ole Moses, an duh view o' duh Promis'
                Lan'
All done 'veal duh scripturs tuh me lack duh Mastuh hab
                'em plan.
Heabunly Choir, sing on in Glory--dyin' now won't be so
                hea'd,
Since ah's seed duh great Green Pasturs an' done heerd duh
                voice o' duh Lawd.

Aunt Sophie Advises (Better Min' Yo' Tongue)

What you been say sistuh Johnson?
De germans is marchin' on;
Better be peel dem yaller yams
'N put dat stew meat on
Better min' yo tongue!
Dat air part de body
Dey been call boneless ham
Been git you kill fer nothin'
Been git you in a jam,
Better min' yo' tongue!
You baine heah 'bout dat doctuh
What been say Hitler win
Done be take from is office
By some gov'mint men?
Better min' yo' tongue!
It been few weeks las' Saddy
Lil Jackson, gal by me
Git rested
'bout some words let slip
While pourin' Buckra's tea,
Better min' yo tongue!
It been what happens Monday;
Dat been de time I saw;
De Law pick Emma boss-man up
Fer been talk 'bout duh Wah,
Better min'yo' tongue!
You know dem Japs sho be a pain;
Beats evuhthing I see,
Mah God-a-mighty—lemme shut mah mouf;
Dey'll come an' git po'me,
Better min' mah tongue!

Race

Chile, is ah glad to see yo' face;
Set down honey--lemme tell you 'bout Race;
Race jes messin' up evuhday--
'Barrasin' deyse'f evuh whichuhway.
Seem lack dat wherebesumevuh dey go
Race got tuh put on uh Minstul Show;
Dey gits on duh Busses an' blows dey top

I
An' fergits all 'bout duh word call "Stop."
Dey lays out dey Boss-womens--talks 'bout dey mens
Lambasts duh prechuhs an' lorates dey frien's.
Honey, is ah glad to see you' face;
Don't go yit—lemme tell you 'bout Race.
One night las' week, b'lieve 'twas Thursday fer sho
Mah boss-woman ast me if ah care to go
To hear Ma'an Anderson sing a song,
An' ah tell her "yassum ah'll go erlong."
Well, honey, yuh knows dat Ma'an am tall
An' duh li'l' white Music man he kinda small;
Well duh minnit dat Ma'an lead duh li'l' man in
Race take notice an' Race staa't tuh grin,
Dey glad fer tuh see Ma'an in front
Uh leadin' dat li'l' bitty ball headed runt;
Dey think dat evuhthing goin' allright
Cause uh nigguh woman leadin' uh man dat's white,
Dey ack lack dis be duh fustes time,
Dat a nigguh have uh white man taggin' behin'
But if'n Race had jest looked aroun' an' see
Dey'd uh know'd dey's wrong by lookin' at me,
Dey'd uh seen't ah's uh cross twixt duh white an' duh black
Cause uh white man follered mah gran'ma way back,
Chile! Is ah glad to see yo' face.
Lemme finish up now tellin' yuh 'bout Race,

Well, Race got uh speshul way hit clap
By takin' dey shoe heel an' toe an' tap
All on duh flo' in duh Singin' Hall
Lack dey wuz havin' uh regluh Ball,
Race aint enjoy duh songs do fine
Dey got duh li'l' Music man on dey min'—
So evuh time dat Ma'an quit
Race staa't tuh clappin' lack dey have uh fit.
Dey lack tuh see duh li'l' man follow,
Ma'an so much, 'till dey laff and holler,
Duh li'l' man's coat hng down in two prongs
An' lack tuh drag duh flo' hit wuz so long;
So Race hit lack duh li'l' man's style
A Walkin' 'hin' Ma'an all duh while,
So, dey claps so loud, till dey haftuh cum back;
An' Race hit laff 'till hit's sides mos' crack.
Ah'm tellin' you honey, hit's us sho disgrace
If youse caught out in public somewhar wid Race,
Cause Race wont only use duh word call Nigguh,
But Race'll flash uh razor an' pull uh trigger.
Honey is ah glad to see yo' face,
See yuh tomorruh at yo' Boss-Man's place.

Pick and Shovel

Bes' friend ah got's dis pick an' shovel;
Warn't fer dem ah'd go barefooted in duh summahtime an'
　　freeze tuh deaf in duh wintuh time.

Know sumpin—dis pick an' shovel sumpin lack life hitse'f;
Hit's uh up an' down thing all duh time jes lack life;
Fus, de pick, he go way down in duh groun' an' loosen up
　　duh dirt; den duh shovel he cum right 'long behin' him
　　an' th'ow duh dirt right back up whar 'twas in duh
　　fus place.

When ah's low in sperrits an' uh stannin' down in duh pit
　　of uh hole ah's done dug out, ah picks up mah shovel
　　what been layin' idle whilst ah stole a whiff fum "Ole
　　Smoky" mah pipe an' ah staa'ts tuh th'owin' dirt outen
　　duh hole up tuh duh groun' ergin, an' jes lack dat ah
　　feels lack uh king o'uh president, o' sumpin some count.
Bes frien' ah's got's dis pick an' shovel.

Pick an' shovel dig uh foundation fer duh skyscraper tuh
　　stan' on so 'twont fall down;
Pick an shovel buil' uh foundation fer mah soul tuh stan' on,
　　too, so's hit kin rise to'a'ds duh glore lan' lack duh
　　skyscraper.

JOHN MASON BREWER: A BIBLIOGRAPHY

BOOKS

Texas

_____. *Echoes of Thought.* 1922. Fort Worth: Progressive Printing Co., 1922.

_____. *Glimpses of Life.* Fort Worth: Progressive Printing Co., 1923.

_____. *Negrito: Negro Dialect Poems of the Southwest.* San Antonio: Naylor, 1933.

_____. *Negro Legislators of Texas and Their Descendants: A History of the Negro in Texas Politics from Reconstruction to Disfranchisement.* Dallas: Mathis Publishing, 1935.

_____, ed. *Heralding Dawn: An Anthology of Verse by Texas Negroes.* Dallas: June Thomason Printing, 1936.

_____. *The Negro in Texas History.* Dallas: Mathis Publishing, 1936.

_____, ed. *Patriotic Moments; A Second Book of Verse.* Dallas: privately printed, 1936.

_____, ed. *A History of the Dallas High School for Negroes.* 1938. Dallas: Friends of the Dallas Public Library, 1991.

_____. *John Wesley Anderson: A Life in Verse.* Dallas: Clyde C. Cockrell & Sons, 1938.

_____, ed. *An Historical Outline of the Negro in Travis County.* Austin: Samuel Huston College, 1940.

_____. *Little Dan from Dixie-Land.* Dallas: Bookcraft, 1940.

_____. *More Truth Than Poetry.* Austin: privately printed, 1947.

_____, ed. *Silhouettes of Life: A Group of Short Stories.* Austin: Samuel Huston College, 1948.

_____. *A Pictorial and Historical Souvenir of Negro Life in Austin, Texas, 1950–51: Who's Who and What's What.* Austin: privately printed, 1951.

_____. *The Word on the Brazos: Negro Preacher Tales from the Brazos Bottoms of Texas*. Austin: University of Texas Press, 1953.

_____. *Aunt Dicy Tales: Snuff-Dipping Tales of the Texas Negro*. Austin: J. Mason Brewer, 1956.

_____. *Dog Ghosts and Other Texas Negro Folk Tales*. Austin: University of Texas Press, 1958.

Non-Texas

Brewer, J. Mason. *American Negro Folklore*. New York: New York Times Book Company, 1968.

_____. *Humorous Folktales of the South Carolina Negro*. Orangeburg, SC: Claflin College Press, 1945.

_____. *Three Looks and Some Peeps*. Salisbury, NC: privately printed, 1963.

_____. *Worser Days and Better Times*. Chicago: Quadrangle Books, 1965.

General Editor, Negro Heritage Series

Adventures of an African Slaver, Being a True Account of the Life of Captain Theodore Conot. Austin: Pemberton Press, 1969.

Memoirs of Elleanore Eldridge. Austin: Pemberton Press, 1969.

Memorials Presented to the Congress of the United States for Promoting the Abolition of Slavery. Austin: Jenkins Publishing, 1970.

The Missionary Pioneer: Or a Brief Memoir of the Life, Labors, and Death of John Stewart. Austin: Pemberton Press, 1969.

ARTICLES

Brewer, J. Mason. "Afro-American Folklore." *Journal of American Folklore* 60 (1947): 377-383.

_____. "American Negro Folklore." *Phylon* 6 (1945): 354-61.

_____. "A Negro Cowboy: J. H. Brewer," in *American Negro*

Folklore, edited by J. Mason Brewer (New York: New York Times Books, 1968), 275-278.

———. "Animal Tales as Told by African Students of Livingstone College." *North Carolina Folklore* 16 (May 1968).

———. "Introduction." *Encyclopedia of Black Folklore and Humor*, edited by Henry D. Spalding. New York: Jonathan David, 1994. Pp. ix-x.

———. "John Tales." *Mexican Border Ballads and other Lore*, edited by Modie C. Boatright. Austin: Texas Folklore Society, 1946. Pp. 81-104.

———. "Juneteenth." *Tone the Bell Easy*, edited by J. Frank Dobie. Austin: Texas Folklore Society, 1932: 9-54.

———. "More of the *Word on the* Brazos." *Observations & Reflections on Texas Folklore*, edited by Francis Edward Abernethy. Dallas: Southern Methodist University Press, 1972: 91-99.

———. "The Negro and the Texas Centennial Exposition." *The Houston Informer.* August 8, 1936, sec. 2, p. 4.

———. "Negro Folklore in North America: A Field of Research." *New Mexico Quarterly* 17 (1946): 27-33.

———. "North Carolina Negro Oral Narratives." *North Carolina Folklore* 9 (July 1961): 21-33.

———. "Old Time Negro Proverbs." *Spur-of-the-Cock*, edited by J. Frank Dobie. Austin: Texas Folklore Society, 1933: 101-105.

———. "Tales from *Juneteenth*." *The Folklore of Texan Cultures*, edited by Francis Edward Abernethy. Austin: The Encino Press, 1974: 115-118.

———. "Texas Negro Tales." *Interracial Review* (December 1959), 236-237.

BIBLIOGRAPHY RELATED TO BREWER

Abernethy, Francis E. "African-American Folklore in Texas and in the Texas Folklore Society." In *Juneteenth Texas: Essays in African-American Folklore*. Edited by Francis E. Abernethy, Patrick B. Mullen, and Alan B. Govenar. Denton, Texas: University of North Texas Press, 1996. Pp. 1-13.

Bacon, Jacqueline. "Imperiled: The Historical J. Mason Brewer Home." *American Visions* 14.6 (1999): 44 +.

Baker, Jr., Houston A. "Black Folklore and the Black American Literary Tradition." In *Long Black Song: Essays in Black American Literature and Culture*. Charlottesville: University Press of Virginia, 1972. Pp. 18-41.

Bontemps, Arna, and Langston Hughes. *The Book of Negro Folklore*. New York: Dodd, Mead, and Co., 1958. Pp. 65-88, 141-53.

"Brewer, John Mason." *Who's Who in America*, 39th ed. (1975).

Brookes, Stella Brewer. *Joel Chandler Harris—Folklorist*. Athens: University of Georgia Press, 1950.

Byrd, James W. *J. Mason Brewer: Negro Folklorist*. Austin: Steck-Vaughn Company, 1967.

_____. "In Memory of John Mason Brewer (1896-1975)." *CLA Journal* 18 (June 1975): 578-81.

_____. "John Mason Brewer." *The Handbook of Texas Online* (http://www.tshaonline.org/handbook/online).

_____. "Dr. J. Mason Brewer." In *Features and Fillers: Texas Journalists on Texas Folklore*, edited by Jim Harris. Denton: University of North Texas Press, 1999. Pp. 168-171.

_____. "Black Collectors of Black Folklore: An Update on Zora Neale Hurston and J. Mason Brewer." *Louisiana Folklore Miscellany* 6.2 (1986): 1 +.

Crowley, Daniel J. "Negro Folklore, an Africanists View." *Texas Quarterly* 5 (1962): 65-71.

Dobie, J. Frank. "A Word on *The Word*," in J. Mason Brewer, *The Word On the Brazos: Negro Preacher Tales From the Brazos Bottoms of Texas*. Austin: University of Texas Press, 1953. Pp. vii-xi.

Dundes, Alan, ed. "J. Mason Brewer, 'Old Time Negro Proverbs.'" In *Mother Wit from the Laughing Barrel: Readings in the Interpretation of Afro-American Folklore*. Jackson: University Press of Mississippi, 1990. Pp. *246-250*.

Galloway, Andy. "Anderson, John Wesley." *The Handbook of Texas Online* (http://www.tshaonline.org/handbook/online).

Glasrud, Bruce A. "African Americans and Texas Folklore." In *Celebrating 100 Years of the Texas Folklore Society, 1909-2009*, edited by Kenneth L. Untiedt. Denton: University of North Texas Press, 2009. Pp. 157-175.

Glasrud, Bruce A. "From Griggs to Brewer: A Review of Black Texas Culture, 1899-1940." *Journal of Big Bend Studies* 15 (2003): 195-212.

Glasrud, Bruce A. "John Mason Brewer." *BlackPast Online Encyclopedia* (http://www.blackpast.org).

Glasrud, Bruce A., and Laurie Champion. "Zora Neale Hurston: Folklorist and Storyteller." In *The Human Tradition in America Between the Wars, 1920-1945*, edited by Donald W. Whisenhunt. Wilmington, Del.: Scholarly Resources, 2002. Pp. 21-31.

Levine, Lawrence W. *Black Culture and Black Consciousness: Afro-American Folk Thought from Slavery to freedom*. New York: 1977.

Milling, Chapman J. "Foreword." *Dog Ghosts and Other Texas Negro Folk Tales*. Austin: University of Texas Press, 1958. Pp. xi-xiv.

Phillips, Michael. "North Texas's Black Art and Literature during the 1920s and 1930s: 'The Current Is Much Stronger.'" In *The Harlem Renaissance in the American West: The New Negro's Western Experience*, edited by Bruce A. Glasrud and Cary D. Wintz. New York: Routledge, 2012. Pp. 27-43.

Sapper, Neil G. "Black Culture in Urban Texas: A Lone Star Renaissance." *Red River Valley Historical Review* 6 (Spring 1981): 56-77. Reprinted in *The African American Experience in Texas*, edited by Bruce A. Glasrud and James M. Smallwood. Lubbock: Texas Tech University Press, 2007. Pp. 231-257.

Spalding, Henry D. "Plantation to Emancipation." *Encyclopedia of Black Folklore and Humor*, edited by Henry D. Spalding. New York: Jonathan David, 1994. Pp. 71-157.

Thomas, Lorenzo. "The African-American Folktale and J. Mason Brewer." In *Juneteenth Texas: Essays in African-American Folklore*. Edited by Francis E. Abernethy, Patrick B. Mullen, and Alan B. Govenar. Denton, Texas: University of North Texas Press, 1996. Pp. 222-235.

Turner, Darwin T. "J. Mason Brewer: Vignettes." *CLA Journal* 18 (June 1975): 570-577.

Turner, Kenneth W. "Negro Collectors of Negro Folklore: A Study of J. Mason Brewer and Zora Neale Hurston. Master's thesis, East Texas State University, 1964.

White, Sandra Flowers. "J. Mason Brewer: An American Folklorist from Texas." Master's thesis, University of Houston-Clear Lake, 1997.

—Bruce A. Glasrud and Milton S. Jordan

www.ingramcontent.com/pod-product-compliance
Lightning Source LLC
Chambersburg PA
CBHW030313080526
44584CB00012B/549